The Streets Are Talking to Me

The publisher and the University of California Press Foundation gratefully acknowledge the generous support of the Ahmanson Foundation Endowment Fund in Humanities.

The Streets Are Talking to Me

to Me

Affective Fragments in Sisi's Egypt

MARIA FREDERIKA MALMSTRÖM

UNIVERSITY OF CALIFORNIA PRESS

University of California Press, one of the most distin-
guished university presses in the United States, enriches
lives around the world by advancing scholarship in the
humanities, social sciences, and natural sciences. Its
activities are supported by the UC Press Foundation and
by philanthropic contributions from individuals and
institutions. For more information, visit www.ucpress.edu.

University of California Press
Oakland, California

© 2019 by Maria Frederika Malmström

Library of Congress Cataloging-in-Publication Data

Names: Malmström, Maria Frederika, 1969– author.
Title: The streets are talking to me : affective fragments
    in Sisi's Egypt / Maria Frederika Malmström.
Description: Oakland, California : University of
    California Press, [2019] | Includes bibliographical
    references and index. |
Identifiers: LCCN 2019014744 (print) | LCCN 2019017604
    (ebook) | ISBN 9780520973046 (e-book) |
    ISBN 9780520304321 (cloth : alk. paper) |
    ISBN 9780520304338 (pbk. : alk. paper)
Subjects: LCSH: Egypt—Politics and government—21st
    century. | Egypt—History—Protests, 2011–2013. |
    Islam and politics—Egypt. | Protest movements—
    Arab countries. | Social movements—Egypt.
Classification: LCC ADT107.88 (ebook) | LCC .M355 2019
    ADT107.88 (print) | DDC 962.05/6—dc23
LC record available at https://lccn.loc.gov/2019014744

Manufactured in the United States of America

27   26   25   24   23   22   21   20   19
10   9   8   7   6   5   4   3   2   1

To my father

In Pietà repose
draped over her right arm
that held this young man's head
    more than concussed
    though no less caressed
wasn't his flowing hair
but was his spilling brains
that she noted alarmed
half-mocking the half-truth
of the wild brevity
of lust, as her very
being's tensile mistrust
shook and then let flow free
as would an untimely
spring in black mid-winter
release a flooding brook.

E. Valentine Daniel

On a summer's night in his Manhattan apartment, when I relayed a painful
lived experience of one of my Cairene friends (from 2011), to my New York
friend and colleague, Professor E. Valentine Daniel, he scribbled out a poem
that contained (in both senses of that word) the essence of the said and the
unsaid of the scene in this verse

Contents

Illustrations

Acknowledgments

To all of you who made this book possible, I would like to express my gratitude from the bottom of my heart. A special thanks to my Cairene friends, "constructed" family, and acquaintances in Egypt. I would love to name you one by one, but you know that it would not be very wise. However, I thank you one by one. You are incredible. I would also like to highlight and give my thanks to all things, places, and spaces that also made this book possible.

A thousand thanks to all my colleagues within academia who were with me from the early stages of the project and those I worked with in the workshops following the project, when I was still was in the middle of fieldwork: I was the convener of the first one, "Affective Politics in Transitional North Africa: Imagining the Future," organized and funded by the Nordic Africa Institute, Uppsala, and the Swedish Institute, Alexandria, Egypt, May 27–28, 2013. The invited participants were Aymon Kreil, Carl Rommel, Dida Badi, Igor Cherstich, Mark Westmoreland, Mohammed Tabishat, Mustafa Aattir, Nefissa Naguib, Samuli

Schielke, Susanne Dahlgren, Senni Jyrkiäinen, and Zakaria Rhani. The second one, "Materiality of Affect in North Africa: Politics in Flux," I convened together with Deborah Kapchan, organized and funded again by the Nordic Africa Institute and New York University, October, 3–4, 2014. The invited participants were Hisham Aidi, Aomar Boum, Vincent Crapanzano, Michael Frishkopf, Farha Ghannam, Jane Goodman, Richard Jankowsky, Susann Ossman, Stefania Pandolfo, Zakia Salime, Paul Silverstein, Ted Swedenburg, Jessica Winegar, Mark LeVine, Abdelmajid Hannoum, and Lila Abu-Lughod. The third workshop, "The Means of Love in the Arab World: Pragmatics beyond Norms and Transgressions," was convened by Aymon Kreil, Samuli Schielke, Zakaria Rhani, and me, organized and funded by the Nordic Africa Institute; Centre Jacques Berque, Rabat; EGE, University Mohammed VI Polytechnique, Rabat; UFSP Asien und Europa, University of Zurich, Zurich; and Zentrum Moderner Orient, Berlin, in Rabat, Morocco, December 11–13, 2015. The invited participants were Annelies Moors, Matthew Carey, Annerienke Fioole, Nico Staiti, Jamal Bammi, Sihem Benchekroun, Nadje Al-Ali, Mériam Cheikh, Sandra Nasser El-Dine, Corinne Fortier, and Luca Nevola.

My heartfelt thanks go to those who were there for me during this life changing journey: those who gave me advice and safety from afar during dangerous situations in field, those with whom I have discussed the early book manuscript and who have encouraged and supported me, and those who read various drafts and approached me with fruitful comments and critiques. These scholars are Mats Utas, Aymon Kreil, David Scott, Talal Asad, Arjun Appadurai, Deborah Kapchan, Farha Ghannam, Amro Ali, Valentine E Daniel, Lila Abu-Lughod, Jessica Winegar, Joseph Frimpong, Mark LeVine, Leif Stenberg, Jonas Otterbeck, Ulrika Trovalla, Eric Trovalla, Anja Frank, Jonas Frykman, Maja Povrzanović Frykman, Emily Martin, Rayna Rapp, Beth Baron, Marianne Hirsch, Laura Ciolkowski, Abou Farman, Maria Vesperi, Carl Rommel, Samuli Schielke, Maria Vesperi, and Marc Michael.

The research for this book and writing of it were made possible by research positions at the Center for Middle Eastern Studies at Lund University and the Nordic Africa Institute, Uppsala, by visiting positions at Columbia University and New York University, and by the three-year grant from Vetenskapsrådet (the Swedish Research Council), the five-year grant from Formas (a Swedish Research Council for Sustainable Development) and the three-year grant from Riksbankens Jubileumsfond (the Bank of Sweden Tercentenary Foundation).

Special warm thanks to my editor, Niels Hooper, and my editorial assistant, Robin Manley, who have believed in my work from the very beginning, and to my brilliant copy editor, Gary J. Hamel, and to the Center for Middle Eastern Studies student Rebecca Irvine, who have assisted me and transformed the manuscript into the correct format.

This book could not have been written without the love, joy, sorrow, and support from my partners in crime, beloved ones, family, and kindred spirits, not only the ones living in Cairo and Alexandria, but in New York City, in different cities in Sweden, and in other parts of the global village. You know who you are. Especially you, my thriving honey daughter, Embla.

Maria Frederika Malmström
New York City, January 25, 2019

Preface

AFTER THE 2011 REVOLTS: LOVING THE SOIL, THE MAN, AND THE COUNTRY

I met him through a friend when I was in Cairo for a short period after the uprisings in 2011. We immediately talked politics in an intense, agitated way, and I did not even recognize my researcher self, always trying to stay a bit politically "distanced" to be able to build trust. This was the beginning of an intense communication between us that continued when I was back in Sweden, through phone, email, and social media. We worked together academically, and I asked him about political flows I did not understand from afar.

When I started my longer fieldwork during the spring of 2013, something else happened. During this period, there was a lot of energy, irritation, disappointment in the political air, but also a new hope among the political opposition. It was a public climate where you could hear taxi drivers complaining out loud, where liberals and others increasingly began to explicitly resist Morsi's rule, and when the Tamarod movement became increasingly active.[1]

When we met again during the spring of 2013, we could sense not only the dominant public mood in Cairo, but also another new one vibrating between us. Intense. There was no beginning and no end. People around us could sense our shared force, filled with heated political discussions, energy, and analysis, but there was also something else there; there was a new, growing electricity. I was surprised. He was too. We continued to hang out, because we could not resist, although the private situation did not allow us to act upon the increasing pulsating desire between us. This was a period in Egypt when there were electricity cuts all the time. It was also a very hot spring. We met one evening at a popular restaurant downtown for dinner and we ordered some full-bodied red wine to begin our passionate political conversations. It was suddenly pitch black in the room as well as extremely hot. One of those electricity cuts. I could feel the sweat beginning to drip from my forehead, back, arms, and I could see the same thing happening to him. The electricity came back for a short while, then another cut, and then again. The increasing heat, the sweat, the pheromones, the heavy red wine, the political conversations, the influence of both inorganic and organic things that flow between us, in combination with the collective emotions of Egypt at that time. Everything pulsated and moved. Exploded. Due to private circumstances, and intimate links to regimes of power at a very high level, I will halt here.

THE DAY BEFORE THE ANNIVERSARY OF THE JANUARY 25 REVOLUTION IN 2014: THE BOMB

In 2014, the day before the anniversary of the January 25 revolution, Leyla's daughter, Shams, slept over.[2] We embraced one of those cozy nights where we shared a bedroom, experiences, and thoughts. As was her wont on such occasions, dressed in one of her bright nightgowns, she sank cozily into the sofa that was covered with a soft, apricot-and-pink flowered fabric that I loved so much. As she reclined, she pulled the blankets up to her nose. I positioned myself on my bed so we could still have eye contact while we talked. I do not remember what Egyptian music we listened to this night, but I do remember that what we listened to emerged from her computer's long list of songs. Even though fatigue threatened to overcome us, we did not want anything, including sleep, to break the special affect that flowed between and through us that night. The new day dawned upon us with an unannounced suddenness. We finally tried to allow ourselves to let go for a few hours and get some sleep. But it was impossible for me to do so, and Shams seemed to be in the same state that I was. So we began to talk again. After an hour or so, we tried again. But sleep was no match for the intensity of our fine-tuned harp of nerves. Given how exhausted I was, I observed, but in silence, that Shams was busy with her computer instead of trying to sleep. I sensed that something was going to happen. She would tell me later how she too had experienced a similar energy. Later, that same day, when I talked with other friends living in Greater Cairo, I learned that several of them had also sensed something similar. Back to the moment: Shams closed her computer screen and put it on the floor, and darkness shrouded the room again, even though we could see the light from the dawn outside sneak through the wooden slats of the blinds. Once again, we tried to force ourselves into sleep, but this time with increasing heartbeats. Perhaps twenty minutes to half an hour went by. We were not at all prepared for what came next. An extremely loud blast of sound shook every cell of our bodies. Without even a second's thought, in a shared instant, we rushed out to the balcony. We could see a gigantic black cloud loom before of us in the city. I shot a photo with my cell phone and, again, without a moment's thought, disseminated it on social media. We understood instantly and simultaneously that the boom we had experienced was from the explosion of a massive bomb. The blast was heard even in Zamalek and elsewhere in Greater Cairo. It was only the first in a series of bombs in Cairo; four the first day and one the day after. The first bomb was a large truck bomb that attacked the police headquarters. The front of the building was severely damaged, as were the National Archives building and the Museum of Islamic Art.

JANUARY 25, 2014: THE DAY OF DEATH AND THE NIGHT OF VODKA

The day after, my friend (and self-proclaimed "bodyguard") Mohamad waited for me downstairs, and we walked together to a building in front of Tahrir Square. I realized after a couple of minutes that I had forgotten my charger and wanted to head back to the apartment, since it is crucial for me that my daughter always be able to reach me wherever I am. We tried several times to go back, but we were stopped each time either by an approaching running crowd, shootings, tear gas, or a combination of all three. During these attempts to get back to the apartment I once began to run, instead of walking as I knew I should do, but Mohamad repeatedly told me, in a sharp but calm voice, to slow down and walk. He helped me to navigate and select safer streets, alleys, or corners to avoid the mobs and shootings, something he was good at, not least due to his political activities in the city during the uprisings in 2011. But Leyla phoned twice, telling me to stay away; they were shooting in the streets outside our apartment. Later that day we figured out that two members of the April 6 movement were shot dead close to my downtown home.

Despite all this violence going on only a few minutes away, in Tahrir Square, where the media was located, we found a kind of "performance" going on—soldiers helping older people or talking to families and playing with their children, while a large crowd chanted in favor of the military. (Rumors circulated at the time that these pro-Sisi people had come in large buses from the countryside and were paid by the regime to act vocally in the square). On one of the many occasions this day that I climbed a fragile ladder (and passed through a poor but welcoming family's home) and went out to the rooftop, I suddenly heard the crowd cheering as military helicopters threw out bundles of Egyptian flags all over the square. For me it looked like a bombing; for the supporters, I suppose, it was more like a material promise of national stability.

That evening, everything calmed down and we could finally get home to get my charger, although we had to escape some running crowds of young men. It was dark, and the streets were dirty. We came upon small fires and a lot of garbage all the way back home. Leyla waited with hot, sweet cups of tea, and I could at last charge my phone. After that, despite Leyla's anxious warnings, we headed back to the popular Syrian coffee shop downtown, where I was supposed to meet other friends and then attend a sleepover party in Dokki. Mohamad headed back to his family, and I sat down for a moment for another tea and a chat with my friends to update each other on the situation. They told me among other things that the police had detained several of our mutual friends at the same coffee shop a couple of hours earlier. Now everything was calm, but of course we could not trust the street; the security could come back at any moment. My ex-husband, an artist from Sweden who was editing our film *Egypt in Motion* at that time, texted me about some editing concern, and I walked a couple of blocks away and called him back. It was a strange decision, but it was like although my body was on fire, I was at the same time very efficient and productive. My thinking capacity was strangely clear as glass; I gave my suggestions for a better edit in the middle of that dark dangerous street and then went back to more political discussions with my friends. After a while, we tried to grab a taxi, but it was hard to get a ride from downtown to Dokki at this moment. Several refused, and when we found one willing taxi driver, the trip was of course much more expensive than usual. The city was dark, empty, and calm. We were all quiet, except for the recitations from the taxi driver's radio. At last, we entered the home of one of my friends. The house was already filled with young women and men. Some of them chatted, another group watched an old movie. It was calm, a much slower pace than the extreme motion during the day. Snacks, soft drinks, and local vodka were offered. Despite drinking much more than I usually do, I did not feel any change, and the same went for my friends. It was like the alcohol could not transform our bodies. We stayed totally sober the whole night. However, the transmission of love clearly calmed our tense bodies.

LATE SUMMER AND FALL 2016: THE FATIGUE COLLECTIVE BODY

Fatiguefatiguefatiguefatiguefatiguefatiguefatiguefatiguefatigue
fatiguedrainedfatiguefatiguefatiguefatiguefatiguefatiguefatiguef
atiguedespairfatiguefatiguefatiguefatiguefatiguefatiguefatigue
depressionfatiguefatiguefatiguefatiguefatiguefatiguefatiguef

atiguepinionedfatiguefatiguefatiguefatiguehopelessnessfatigue
fatiguefatiguemutedfatiguefatiguefatiguefatiguefatiguefatiguef
atiguefatiguefatiguelossfatiguefatiguefatiguefatiguefatigue
fatiguefatigueguiltfatiguefatiguefatiguefatiguefatiguefatiguef
atiguefailurefatiguefatiguefatigueangerfatiguefatiguefatigue
fatiguepainfatiguefatiguefatiguefatigueabsencefatiguefatiguef
atiguefatiguesuppressedfatiguefatiguefatiguefatiguedisapperanc
efatiguefatiguefatiguefatiguefatiguefatiguefatiguefatiguesilence
dfatiguefatiguefatiguefatiguefatiguefatiguefatiguefatiguefatigu
eworriedfatiguefatiguefatiguefatigueleavingfatiguefatiguef
atiguedeathfatiguefatiguefatiguefatiguefatiguefatiguefatigue
fatiguefatiguestuckfatiguefatiguefatiguefatiguefatiguefatiguef
atiguefatiguetorturefatiguefatiguedenialfatiguefatiguefatigue
fatiguefatiguefatiguefatiguefatiguefatiguefatiguefatigueinsecur
efatiguefatiguefatiguefatiguefatiguetraumafatiguefatiguefatig
uefatiguefatiguecombatfatiguefatiguefatiguefatiguefatiguefatigu
efatiguefatiguefatiguefatiguefatiguefatiguefatiguefatiguefatig
uefatiguedecrepitfatigfatiguefatiguefatiguefatiguefatiguefatigu
efatiguescaredfatiguefatiguefatiguefatiguefatiguefatiguefatiguef
atiguefatigueemptinessfatiguefatiguefatiguefatiguefatiguefatigu
efatiguefatiguefatiguefatiguefatiguefatiguefatigueboredomf
atiguefatiguefatiguefatiguefatiguefatiguefatiguefatiguefatigue
fatiguepovertyfatiguefatiguefatiguefatiguefatiguefatiguefatig
uefatiguefatiguefatiguefatiguefatiguefatiguefatiguefatiguefati
guefatiguefatiguefatiguefatiguE. (Malmström, September 2016)

Conducting fieldwork in Cairo during the fall of 2016 was one of the most demanding things I had ever done—until I came back one year later. It was even worse in 2017 and 2018. In huge contrast to the intense, affective, uncertain, sometimes violent fieldwork of the previous couple of years, I believe this period reached its peak in something totally different, which was a very specific and overwhelmingly negative public body of affect that began after President Sisi came to power. The difference is interesting, since the earlier experiences were much more acute and often dangerous, but, at the same time, filled with imagination, hope, rapid motion, and a collective imagination of a potential new Egypt. This period during 2016 was filled instead with a lack of energy, a boredom, and also with a sense of loss, in combination with a paranoid military dictatorship's tactics to control its citizens via a collapse of the everyday economy and a total repression of political bodies, which produced a public depression and an everyday anxiety, heavily transmitted between bodies, including the body of the researcher.[3] After a few weeks in Cairo I adapted quite well, or maybe not, depending on how to understand the research scenario, fieldwork, and analysis. I felt cautious and pinioned, but most of all, the fatigue and gloomy atmosphere were extremely demanding. I felt more exhausted than ever before in the field, and like the Egyptians I hang out with, increasingly depressed.

After a trip to Dahab for several days to cheer up with some Cairene friends, I decided not to go back with them to Cairo, but to stay for a few days extra to regain strength. The plan was to travel to Suez after that, where I had been invited by a family I know to celebrate Eid el-Adha with them. However, I felt an absolute unhappiness and lack of energy during the day and dreamed intense nightmares during the night. My researcher/ private body slept for eleven hours per night, but I was still forced to take a daily siesta for another one and a half hours during the day. I decided to stay for another ten days. I planned to write a draft about what I had experienced the previous couple of weeks. I tried to write some work-in-progress texts. It was impossible. I was stuck. I was drained, but, again, as I elaborate in chapter 4, I could leave Cairo for more than ten days of calmness in Dahab, or leave the country if I wished, in contrast to many of the Egyptians I knew. I felt an abstract sense of loss, but again, it was not my own; it was more a sensorial circulation between the bodies of Cairenes I knew and did not know. The experience was intense and powerful. I could feel others' pain, others' depression, but I could not write.

FROM FALL 2017 TO WINTER 2018: DRINKING STELLA BEER WITH THE INTELLIGENCE

This was in the early afternoon, my second day in Cairo in 2017. I did some errands before catching up with Fatma at a local pub. Before beginning to chat we prepared our phones in order to stay as safe as possible. We were calm, but cautious, and most of all, thrilled to meet again. The atmosphere was of joy, happiness, and energy. Nevertheless, very soon thereafter, way too soon, a man entered the pub. He approached us with two Stella (local beers), and I knew from earlier fieldwork that he is a *mukhabarat* (intelligence guy). In a soft and gentle tone, he welcomed me to Egypt, and left the beers for us at a wooden table. Before he left the bar, he informed me that he had seen me earlier during the day in downtown Cairo and gave me the exact name of the streets. Then he left the pub. I froze. This was certainly the beginning of a new era. My body became immediately alert and suspicious, and although I have always been cautious, my body learned novel ways of navigating during this fieldwork period. Fatma sarcastically burst out, but in a low volume, that this guy must have been informed by the intelligence apparatus about my earlier route (someone else had followed me as a shadow) as well as where to find us at the bar. Obviously, she said, his mission was to warn me and let me know that they had their eyes on me. We sipped the *mukhabarat's* beer, but it did not taste as good as it usually does. We had lost our thirst. When I came back to the apartment the same evening, I made a phone call to a scholar abroad (on a safe telephone app). This person is familiar with the current security situation in Egypt. He became very worried. When I heard his anxious voice, in that moment, I became even more uneasy. Like my Cairene friends I did not feel safe at home or in the street. When someone suddenly was knocking on the front door, especially early in the morning or very late, it felt like my heart was beating so heavily that it might explode. (My Cairene friends told me they had a similar reaction.) Back to my friend from abroad. I promised to check in with him a couple of times per day, and he also texted and called me during the first weeks of fieldwork. But nothing else happened. However, like my Cairene fellows, I was more suspicious than ever before. Every move and action had to be thought through in advance. My body was tense and alert for five months, and it took a long while to recover. Shortly after this had happened, I met some other politically active friends in Cairo, who all warned me that the government was hyper-paranoid, even worse than the previous year. They told me to leave all phones at home if I did any interviews, and use VPNs and the like if I used computers for work. They said not to talk politics in quiet public places, to be aware of the surveillance cameras and even recorders in pubs and coffee shops, and constantly be cautious and alert about unknown people observing or taking photos of me and my fellows in public places. In their view, it was an extraordinarily dangerous time in Egypt.

Materiality and Politics of Affect in Egypt

A Study of (Non-)Change Grounded in Empirical Research

MID-AUGUST 2013, DOWNTOWN CAIRO

What becomes of one who dared to simply exist in the aftermath of the largest massacre of demonstrators in protest history?

August 17. The dusty Cairo streets were eerily empty and quiet, as during the 6-to-6 curfew. The mistrust of the uncanny stillness of the streets was palpable. But at last we were able to go out to a totally new city—a ghost city. I helped Leyla for food, since we were out of everything. We managed to buy some groceries, including large amounts of chocolate, despite all the closed shops around us in this new, empty, unfamiliar, and uncertain landscape. At our last stop—a pharmacy only a few

Figure 1. Muslim Brotherhood supporters follow reports of the election broadcast on national radio, June 24, 2012. Courtesy of an anonymous photographer.

Figure 2. Mohamed Morsi of the Muslim Brotherhood was declared Egypt's President, June 24, 2012, and his supporters celebrated in Tahrir Square. Courtesy of an anonymous photographer.

blocks from home—the staff suddenly began locking the doors. They told us and the other few remaining customers that they had heard that there was a mob running right in our direction from the Al-Fath Mosque. At this point, I panicked. Leyla was enfeebled by age and incapable of assuming the hurried stride that the anxious moment called for. Besides, we were far from safe inside the glass-walled store.

The poignant, affective memory of my flight from (and with) a pro-Morsi demonstration in downtown Cairo suddenly broke out like a cold sweat. On that occasion, four days ago, I had almost been unable to run. The tear gas that had burned my eyes and skin, stinging my body, especially my face and neck, had filled my lungs with choking pain. In spite of his own reddening eyes, one of the male demonstrators had taken my hand, and with tears flowing down his cheeks and long black beard, dragged me away from the surging crowd and the white clouds of tear gas. I recalled the touch of his warm hand. I had simultaneously trusted and distrusted him. Against the pull of suspicion, I strove to catch the drift of his navigation so as to make it mine. I was scared, but I needed to rely on an unfamiliar body in motion even as I was overwhelmed by this same body's uncommon concern for my safety. Neither of us could see very well, but we managed to find a safe escape away from the panicked crowd, which was in turn fleeing a pursuing cloud of gas.

Back to the pharmacy. Here, while expecting to face a different agitated mob, something unexpected happened. Leyla's pale face changed from drained to resolute; she looked steadfast. Leyla calculated the exact amount of time we would need to make it home and then said to me, "We'll have time; we still have a few minutes. Come on now, Maria, let us walk home now, *yallah*." Heavily laden with bags of groceries, we made an effort to walk home as fast as possible. We made it, and climbed the many stairs to our floor. Back in the apartment, our frightened bodies soaked in sweat and shivering, we soon realized that this time there had been no need to hurry: it was a false alarm.

Thinking through Vibrant (Non-)Living Materialities

According to Human Rights Watch (2014a), a minimum of 817 people and more likely at least 1,000 were killed in Rabaa' al-Adawiya Square alone on August 14, 2013. As the above ethnographic vignette relates, the days that followed were scary and uncertain, as will be fleshed out further in chapters 3 and 4. The sites Rabaa' al-Adawiya and al-Nahda were occupied by thousands of supporters of the ousted President Mohamed Morsi and others from all parts of Egypt who were critical of the military's political intervention. The sit-ins had begun a few days before June 30 in camps that have been described as well-organized, clean, city-like places, with planned architecture: tents, streets, children's playgrounds, street vendors, sweepers, and security personnel. The protesters were there to oppose the ousting of Morsi, July 3, 2013 (Al Jazeera 2013). Some Egyptians participated in the sit-ins not in support of the Muslim Brotherhood but against the military or in favor of democracy. Other Egyptians—whether they voted for Morsi or not—supported the military on July 3, but are devastated today because of the bloody repression and seizure of power by the military government. There are also Egyptians who opposed both groups and instead formed new political groups or campaigns of resistance after the massacre. One such protest movement whose activities are revealing was Masmou3, a campaign that started after the curfew was imposed. Masmou3 encouraged Egyptians to open their window at nine o'clock every night and beat saucepans, play musical instruments, clap hands, and do whatever else they could to produce noise and sonic resistance. Although this campaign of noise had little success, it was a cacophonic source of resistance against the national masculine soundscape of the military.

The sit-ins consisted of a few thousand protesters who declared themselves to be peaceful but whom the state security and the interim government considered to be an immense threat to the stability of the country. The dispersal of the sit-ins turned out to be the beginning/continuation of the state fight against (global) terrorism. After the dispersal of the sit-ins, General Abdel Fattah Saeed Hussein Khalil al-Sisi, the current president of Egypt, was appointed first deputy prime minister, while remaining minister of defense. He immediately addressed the nation on television about the necessity to fight terrorism, thereby following the strategy of weakening political opposition employed by previous Egyptian state leaders, not least being the Mubarak regime, which "had staked its international legitimacy on its claim to be acting as a bulwark against Islamic fundamentalists, particularly the Muslim Brotherhood" (Hirschkind 2012, 50).

This book is about the story of the aftermath of the "failed revolution" in Egypt and what happened to it, especially after the disaster in 2013, through the prism of affect theory and new materialism (to be further elaborated below). Because the precarious security situation during these years prevented researchers from conducting a structured kind of inquiry, the book deals with fragments of events and attempts to understand the sensory experiences that are bound together in them. It asks questions such as: How are (non-)living materialities, spaces, and places linked together? How do effects (emotions) of affect move between bodies, objects, places, and spaces in relation to time?

In this book, we will meet matter in relation to an imagined or rejected nation. We will meet women and men of different generations more and less politically active. We will meet the (forces of) flows between certain things, spaces, places, and political bodies in relation to frequency and temporalities. We will meet Leyla again, and we will meet Salah, who talked about his chronic feeling of shame, anxiety, and depression made explicit exhibited in his body language, especially in his posture. Salah told me about his friend, whom he had looked upon as his "brother," as family, after spending every minute with him during the intense eighteen days in Tahrir Square, or "Tahrir Country," as he phrased it. Recalling his friend, Salah said, "He jumped up in the air and took the bullet meant for me." Salah's friend was killed in an instant, while Salah himself was still alive. We will meet another young male protestor, Kamal, who, among many others, was shot in the eye by Central Security Forces snipers who from November 2011 onward targeted protestors' heads (see Kingsley 2013). Kamal was still deeply depressed when I talked with him in the winter of 2018. He was convinced that his eye was no longer part of his body; it had been forced to leave his body, he felt, because of the protestors' vast political failure in 2011 and onward. He underscored the non-separation between his individual body and the failure of the revolts. These examples highlight the significance of exploring material affective consequences in relation to the everyday. Affective responses are not static and will most certainly change constantly in accordance with both time and context, which will be elaborated further below as well as through ethnographic examples later on. In this book, I argue that my unit of analysis and methodology enable us to say something about how materialities and affect have contributed to an exaggerated sense of displacement, uncertainty, and tension in Egypt, as well as to a collective and individual loss of hope for an imagined new national home. It also allows us to say something about how affect and materialities work simultaneously toward strengthening people's sense of belonging and public intimacy. As the anthropologist Kathleen Stewart (2007, 2) says, affect "can be experienced as a pleasure and a shock, as an empty pause or a dragging undertow, as a sensibility that snaps into place or a profound disorientation."

THE EPISTEMOLOGICAL TURN

The epistemological turn away from language—in which the focus on affect has emerged as a critique of poststructuralism's inability to recognize the nondiscursive forces that also shape the body—is, in my view, imperative, since using the framework of affect theory and new materialism (described below) allows us to assess politically unstable societies, though only if our material is grounded in empirical research (see Frykman and Povrzanović Frykman [2016] for a rich overview).[1] Scholars often define *affect* as the pre-discursive forces that mold the body, senses, and consciousness. Affect is in this perspective related to, but should not be understood as synonymous with, feelings and emotions. According to several theorists, affect cannot be signified: it is resistant to language and remains in excess to it (Gilje 2016; Blackman and Venn 2010, 9; Massumi 1995, 96; Gregg and Seigworth 2010, 1–2; Shouse 2005). Affect, it is said, "can only be experienced and evoked" (Jansen 2016, 59). Yet it is possible to analyze the effect of these intense forces, as effects of affect (Massumi 1995). I understand affect, drawing on Brian Massumi (1995), as an intense force that can shape and flow through a body/bodies, where it may become tangible and experienced as emotions (Malmström 2014b). The forces of affect that shape the body can be (non-) material, with vast political implications. I am also inspired by one of the most groundbreaking thinkers on affect within anthropology, Kathleen Stewart (2007), who has formulated a novel anthropological mode of writing in which the central objectives are experimentation, speculation, and attunement to potential.

The paradigmatic shift, however, "has cast subjectivity against affect, as if one cancels the other and as if one had to choose between camps of theoretical approach: a subject-centered or an object-oriented one" (Navaro-Yashin 2009, 14). Like other anthropologists such as Yael Navaro-Yashin, I emphasize that our ethnographies may push us to employ a multi-paradigmatic theoretical approach (see Malmström 2014d). Furthermore, using the framework of affect theory and new materialism allows us to assess societies in (or after) flux (see Malmström forthcoming). I, as do other scholars, "claim that ethnographic research provides a fertile ground from which to capture the ambiguities of affective and emotive experience" (Frykman and Povrzanović Frykman 2016, 10). By way of different ethnographic examples and narratives throughout this book, I still interpret meaning, but I also explore affect and new materialism in relation to political bodies in an innovative way that enables me to formulate new questions and thoughts.

MY MODE OF ANALYSIS

As human beings, we inhabit an ineluctably material world. We live our everyday lives surrounded by, immersed in, matter. We are ourselves composed of

matter.... In light of this massive materiality, how
could we be anything other than materialist? How
could we ignore the power of matter and the ways it
materializes in our ordinary experiences or fail to
acknowledge the primacy of matter in our theories?

(Coole and Frost 2010, 1)

To sum up, in this book I deploy a spatially sensitive artifact-oriented anthropology that views things as possessing materiality that determines their affective dimension, changing and transforming people's political bodies—sometimes transgressively so—as they exist in and move through space (Deleuze and Guattari 1987).[2] It explores the complexities of lived experience—that is, the intensities of embodied being in relation to affective energies between living and nonliving matter, space, and place—and aims to increase attention to the felt "texture" of experience (Sedgwick 2003). Exploring how we are affected by and affect our environments is key (see Gregg and Seigworth 2010).

I am especially enthusiastic about the work of the political theorist Jane Bennett (2010, xvii), who puts forward the active role of nonhuman materials in human life (matter itself exhibits agency) and the necessity of adding material agency into the analysis of agential capacity. Her concept of "thing-power" refers to the ability of inorganic and organic things to be more than objects and to manifest independent aliveness as vibrant matter (think, for example, of trash, with countless microscopic organisms), something we will learn more about, especially in chapter 4. She suggests the concept as a way to think beyond the life–matter binary. She also extends her concept of material agency to include the agency of assemblages and collectives, drawing on the philosopher Gilles Deleuze and the psychoanalyst Félix Guattari, where the locus of agency is always a human-nonhuman working group (Bennett 2010), to be compared with the philosopher and anthropologist Bruno Latour's (2004) well-known relational term *actant* (either human or nonhuman—both can act to different degrees depending on levels of power and context) (see also Henare, Holbraad, and Wastell 2007). It may also be good to relate these ideas to the philosopher Thomas Hobbes (in Frost 2010), who perceives everything as material, although some materialities are capable of thoughts—human beings, for example, which he terms "thinking-bodies" (see further in chapter 4). Hobbes also rejects the individual's self-sovereignty. This does not mean a total denial of a person's agential capacity, but rather that individuals "actively foster an illusion of autonomy so that we can *feel* effective when we act" (Frost 2010, 160).

What comes after dramatic experiences (including those that involve trauma, such as revolution or war; see Das [1995] or Kapferer [2015]), may be saturated with a sense of motionlessness, boredom, or loss. Studying the afterlife of uprisings such as those of 2011 through "the flow of objects over time and the simultaneous changes in social memory" (Škrbić Alempijević and Potkonjak 2016, 108) is for me just as important as studying the political uprisings themselves. The researcher will not only be able to explore how the past influences today's political and social actions and creates new affective worlds, but will also be able to sense "'rifts' in affective responses and practices that stand out against the contemporary horizon of values" (Škrbić Alempijević and Potkonjak 2016, 108).

Studying affective politics materialized as emotions might be considered a bit marginal, especially in relation to understanding politics on the macro level and radical changes in the geopolitical map. But I believe that understanding the dynamics of politics should include the theoretical framework of what I term "the materiality of affect," where we as researchers can analyze the forces of affect through their effects, using Massumi's language: tangible manifestations of the multifaceted spectra of ambivalent emotions (see Protevi 2009). Material aspects of public affect in this book means acknowledging the affective power of an object, placing focus on the implicate relationships between the material and affective experiences, one that decenters the traditional focus on individual subjects (but should not be suspended totally, since synesthetic processes are going on somewhere) in favor of exploring how material reality shapes and is shaped by the emotional-aesthetic responses of individuals and groups to the stimuli it provides (see, for example, the ethnographic vignettes).[3] These flows of (non-)living materialities are inherently affective, meaning that specific forces have the ability to flow through and shape the bodies with which, or whom, they come in contact and, through this, the actions in which they engage; they morph continuously, changing valence as they pass from hand to hand, body to body, circumstance to circumstance (see Massumi 1995). The material expressions of these flows and interactions are sites for interrogating, for example, hate and love, which will further be elaborated in chapter 2, two opposed but interlinked "emotions of revolution" used to mark the boundaries of a political community, as well as their sibling, fear. The same material experiences can produce tangible emotions that are mixed, situational, ambivalent, and ambiguous depending on specific political and social positioning within the larger polity or depending on temporality and frequency, as discussed above.

The ethnographic vignettes at the beginning of this introduction allow us to pay attention to the constant uncertainty of the floating everyday life that encompasses intense violent events. They also reveal the intense embodied memories of insecure political bodies, memories that may return in novel contexts (further unfolded throughout this book), which indicate potential societal change or/and trauma. The vignettes also highlight the ethnography of an event and the lived affective experiences among interlocutors as well as among scholars who are conducting fieldwork during and after violent happenings. The transmission of affect (Brennan 2004) during such uncertain moments, from one body to another, tangible as various emotions, is forceful, intense, and demanding. How, then, should we write about the unmentionables with regard to sensationalism, to the interlocutors' security and care, and also to the reader's sensitivities. I believe, as a scholar, it is important to be an uncomfortable pebble in the shoe to a certain extent, but there are sensitive limits. I argue that there is a necessity to include the ugly, the disgusting, the ulcerated—without acting as a voyeur—as well to reveal parts of the private and professional body of the researcher, since both are highly active in the analysis of the research project. The analytical insight given is that with the focus on the materiality of affect we will reach new insights about rapid transformations that unfold during fierce uprisings or military coups, but also the afterlife of such events in relation to both individual and collective political bodies, including the body of the researcher.

COLLABORATIVE RESEARCH AS A TOOL

This book is also an attempt to contribute to scholarship in places that seem unfit for this type of inquiry. Since 2013, as we know, due to the current political constraints in Egypt and the fluidity of affects, it has become extraordinarily arduous to conduct research in Cairo, especially as a foreigner and with the focus on affective politics in relation to (non-)living matter. To overcome these difficulties, I have employed collaborative research as a research tool. These Cairenes have shared their earlier lived experiences, and we shared others together. They have also shared their written texts, photos, films, and music. And they have given me their love, affection, and generosity. These women and men have also protected and encouraged me during these demanding years and have taught me how to navigate more safely. I have moved with my collaborators through, in, and around their cityscape. Moving with them as they drive, walk, travel, or socialize, I have followed how events, actions, and interpretations unfold, as a way to gain an understanding of the very fluid and contradictory material reality that all people are experiencing (Kusenbach 2003). But I have also been attentive to how these women and men talked and expressed feelings, including bodily postures, in relation to how it was—the present—the future. I have paid attention to objects relating to memories, exploring the lingering affective power things still might have for how, for example, memories are preserved and communicated through affective relations to specific objects.

I have also been engaging in "sense walking" (a methodology in which I try to experience the streets in an intersensory way, not focusing on my sight). An intersensory approach (as in synesthesia) is an imperative point of departure if we wish to adequately understand affect, for, as Connor explains, "the senses are multiply related; we rarely if ever apprehend the world through one sense alone" (Connor 2004, 1; see Hsu 2008; Potter 2008). However, I contend that focusing on only one sense at a time, and avoiding sight—sound walking (see LaBelle 2006) as methodology—can be employed as a way to experience changes in the materiality of the affect of vibrations.[4] Even though it is impossible to shut down our other senses, a conscious focus on listening to the alterations of the empirical soundscape is viable (see chapters 3 and 5).[5] This opens up the possibility to listen in to events as they unfold, to the sounds of power and violence, to voices whose testimonies are silenced by dominant narratives, and to cultural expressions of conflict and displacement.[6]

I have known many of my research collaborators since the early 2000s; they are Cairene women and men from different generations, and social strata, most often well-educated, and with different (and often changing) orientations in relation to Islam. Some are secular, some are Sunni, some combine Sufism and communism. For the moment, most identify as Muslims but choose bohemian lifestyles, and a private relationship to God, and are actively negotiating social and religious contexts. They frequently attend local coffee shops and bars in downtown Cairo. The women and men are, in their own view, critical, Left-oriented, and politically aware, sometimes referring to themselves as intellectuals (*mothaaqafoun* for men and *mothaqqafaat* for women) or the new bourgeoisie. They are, for example, poets, writers, filmmakers, actors, musicians, and dancers with various (most often uncertain) incomes, often working at something other than their vocations to be able to survive. Others are journalists, lawyers, scholars, and human rights activists. Hence, their lifestyle and lived experiences, their critical and reflexive thoughts, their artistic ambitions and actions make them into privileged producers of knowledge. These Cairene women and men have shared their multifaceted knowledge with me during the entire project, and this book would not have been written without them. We wrote this book together. Having said that, in light of the politically sensitive nature of the subject matter, I have decided not to provide any further information about my interlocutors in order to ensure them safety.

My fieldwork in Cairo was carried out from part of October 2012, the beginning of May to the end of August 2013 (except for some weeks in June and July), again in January and part of February 2014, in January 2015, in February 2016, from the end of August to the beginning of November 2016, and again from the beginning of September 2017 to the end of January 2018. (I supplemented these field trips with phone calls, conversations via social media and email when I was not in Egypt.) My earlier fieldwork experiences in Cairo are, of course, of value, since I have been able to experience both continuity and change during these years.

OUTLINE OF THE BOOK

This introduction provides a theoretical framing of the questions around affect and new materialism and the aftermath of the "Arab Spring" in Egypt as well as a brief elaboration of my anthropological thinking about the momentous events in the Arab world that began in 2011. To understand the political role of the materiality of affect in Egypt, we need to consider the increasing national fatigue and go back in time: since the beginning of 2011, intense forces of affect have been moving in and out of the bodies of Egyptians in an unfamiliar way (see Bergson 2007). All these intense, frightening, and violent events, as well as those that have been boring or cheerful and peaceful, have deeply affected and transformed Egyptians' political bodies (see Deleuze and Guattari 1987, Massumi 2002). The entire book adds to empirical knowledge about the material as well as affective conditions in Egypt and the constant creation, as well as loss, of national identity, belonging, and citizenship. But each chapter of this book addresses the issue of affect and materiality in a specific way, although in a manner coherent with the other chapters, as presented below.

In chapter 1 we will meet the hurt body and the fake body, and their links to the "Arab Winter" through the narrative of Kamal, who lost his eye in 2011. Chapters 1 and 2 elaborate specifically on how the materiality of affect between self, others, and the country is deeply intertwined in relation to frequency and temporalities. The same (non-)living matter and cityscape produce different forces of affect at different times. These chapters retell the story of the years between 2011 and 2016 and are a teleological attempt to make sense out of them by my collaborators. It offers a bridge to the reader between the 2011 period, which is much studied, and the 2013 period, on which there is much less literature. As mentioned earlier, this is due to the many difficulties and challenges encountered by researchers to conduct fieldwork in Egypt since then.

Chapter 2 engages with experiences of the passionate body, the shameful body, the angry body, the euphoric body, and more. Sometimes the agency of the body moves in directions the self may not desire or be capable of dealing with. It also discusses how love and other emotions are created via the transmission of a public affect of passion and explores today's national sentiments as mutable sentiments that resonate with, and transform in, everyday engagement with the material world. Both chapter 1 and chapter 2 reflect upon how collective political bodies, urban places and spaces, and nonorganic materialities mold and change people in relation to intensity and potentiality.

Chapter 3 discusses sonic affective materiality, especially the lack of sound, during the summer of 2013 in relation to home and displacement. It gives a glimpse of the days and nights with Egyptian friends and collaborators in their homes during the time when Egyptian security forces raided two camps of protesters in Cairo on August 14, 2013. Academia and the media have focused on the movements in the streets and have placed little emphasis on how people were coping with their everyday lives during these intense moments or how the uprisings were lived in the rural areas (exceptions are Winegar [2012] and Abu-Lughod [2012]). Sounds and displacement reflect physical as well as political expulsions from polity and territory: a material as well as affective process that has wide-ranging implications for people's (sense of) safety, belonging, and positionality. The displacement in question is not the movement from one "place" to another, even strange, "place." It is a movement from "place" into a "space." By focusing on the understudied realm of sound, a fresh vantage point is given from which to interrogate the way individuals and collectives experience and navigate the complexities of homemaking during different forms of displacement.

Chapter 4 sets out to explore material aspects of public affect in 2013 in a different way. It examines the role of the agential force of both (non-)organic things and humans and it explores the clearing and dispersals of the Rabaa' al-Adawiya and al-Nahda Cairo sit-ins on August 14, 2013, and what happened through the selected theoretical lens. It gives attention to matter themselves, including both the things of the sit-ins, with a focus on Rabaa' al-Adawiya, and the visible photos of the chapter. The photographer and collaborator of chapter 4 shot these photos at the sit-in of Rabaa' al-Adawiya, and she also composed the captions, as well as wrote a vivid account of her lived experiences in Cairo since 2011.

Chapter 5, the conclusion, recapitulates the elements presented in the book to give a coherent picture of the current situation in Egypt and to show the relevance of the selected theoretical approach. It also brings some new layers of analysis to its object. The chapter examines how the current regime use of the materiality of affect have deeply molded political active bodies. These materialized experiences are connected to how gendered bodies are produced, remade, expressed, and negotiated. However, the current public affect of lack of energy and sense of loss, in combination with a paranoid military dictatorship's tactics to control its citizens via a collapse of the everyday economy and a total repression of political bodies, especially male bodies, produces a public depression and an everyday anxiety that may mold these bodies differently.

Yallah, let us begin our journey through affective politics!

ONE

"Fake Face"

Body, Matter, Cityscape as One

TO BE AFFECTED

… it is to explore the novel potentiality of a
becoming that is always not yet."

(Kapferer 2015, 16)

This chapter will let us further understand, through ethnography, that there is no distinct separation between bodies, things, and cityscapes; instead, these are intimately interconnected—a thick entanglement—and the transmission of affect constantly flows between matter, space, and place. "To experience place is to *be affected by place*, just as it involves an active reckoning of the tactical opportunities and practical resources places invariably present" (Duff 2010, 881). We will also learn more about how temporality and frequency clearly influence these flows. Below, one account is given of how bodies, matter, urban place, and space are deeply and intimately interconnected, how they

Figure 3. Mohamed Mahmoud Street, Cairo, January 10, 2014. Photo by the author.

influence each other, and how the materialization of certain clusters of affect is linked to notions of an imagined new nation or a loss of the same.

KAMAL

Kamal is a friend, in his early thirties and well educated, whom I did not know until quite recently (we met in 2016). Kamal was someone I immediately trusted. He is not only very intelligent but warm and thoughtful. At the very outset of our friendship he started talking about the loss of his eye, including detailed experiences from 2011 up to today. I realized that these experiences were not only intimately linked to his struggles in the 2011 uprisings but were also part of his new self. This account differs from the others in this book, because, although we talked a lot while I was in Cairo, I asked Kamal for an additional written account (where the breaking of time barriers is explicit, but with a predominance of present tense or past continuous tense) of what happened, and I did not change his story, except for language editing.

Part 1

It started with a mild pain in the back of my injured eye, when it was still there. I was flourishing in my work with my dream team; we were achieving an extraordinary target, we were motivated, working very hard for more than ten hours per day, sleeping at the office, and everything was perfect for my burning soul. I thought the pain was a result of work stress, but it began to increase day after day, so I decided to take a break once we finished our plan, and finally we did it. Then I traveled with my friends to Siwa, where we could find rest and peace from our damaging city. It was a great trip, but the pain was still there, preventing me from finding rest or peace, a continuous deep pain irritating a nerve, as if it was burning one of my nerves deep inside my eye.

During the trip, my friend Ahmed, an artist—we went through very dangerous and critical events together during the revolution—recognized my suffering from my being so nervous all the time for no reason, so when we got back home, we went to an eye doctor—she was the one who had tried to arrange medical papers for me to travel outside the country to find a solution for my eye three years earlier—but she told me at that time, "Your eye can't see light anymore, so it will be very hard to be able to see again." Now, when I saw her, she welcomed me warmly; she still remembered me. I told her what I felt, she made her examination through her medical device that I had become expert with, and then she didn't say anything but "hmm." And I remembered this remarkable "hmm," along with a gentle pat on my shoulder, from all the doctors who examined my eye right after the injury. At the time, I had thought it was a minor injury and I would be fine, everything is going to be fine, the most important thing is that our revolution is going to win!

Later on, I understood from them that this "hmm" meant, "You have lost your eye, young man," as one of them told me then. I didn't care; instead I was very proud and took it as a badge of honor. I decided not to tell anyone about it. This is my precious gift; she and I will find our ways through this dark unjust world. She was motivating me when I was very depressed or hopeless; I was motivating others. Even after my first surgery, a patient beside me, who had also lost one of his preciouses, was very depressed after his surgery. I can't forget how his family and mine were very surprised that I was the one who was consoling him. Now, after her "hmm," I felt very deep inside that my precious was going to leave me. The doctor said to me, "Don't worry, it's just inflammations. You take these medications and everything is going to be fine." I said to her, "What if everything doesn't turn out all right?" She replied nervously, as if she knew, "No, everything will be fine. Just take your medication and come back in a week to ..." and started to describe what I should take, but I wasn't really listening. I was *shocked*; my heart was aching so hard that I couldn't hear anything. I was surprised, because I'd known three years earlier that this was going to happen. What was new? Maybe the status of the revolution, maybe what was happening, the anti-revolution powers that came back to destroy everything that the revolution built for the people, and mainly to conquer our freedom.

My friend Ahmed was with me and without any words he drove me to the square, the doctor was two blocks away from it. I was really crying, maybe for the first time, because of my eye. I remember the graffiti that was on the wall of the AUC [American University of Cairo], a young man with a green, lost, challenging eye that looked toward the square, at exactly the same place where the soldier had stood to shoot us.

I went home after I caught my breath and my friend Ahmed told me not to be pessimistic; the doctor said everything is going to be fine. I told my mother about what the doctor told me and she was calm and said, "Thank God, did you buy your medication?" I said, "But I think I will remove it." She replied in a nervous voice, "Don't be dramatic, the doctor said everything will be fine, don't wish for an ordeal!" I wasn't wishing, I was sure that this was going to happen, but no one listened or wanted to listen. That day I wrote a post on Facebook in Arabic:

نعم هي راحلة، لم يكن يتوهم كعادته، لم تعد تتحمل ماتراه، أيقنت أن للصبر حدود، و
حدوده أن ترىقاتلها وهو يتباهى ويحتفل بفجره وظلمه، والجميع يهلل ويسبح بحمده، كا
نت تبصر مالم يبصروه، تئنوتتألم لضمور وموت حلمها وحلم رفقائها المخلصين فى بل
د الوهم والممنوع، كانت على يقين أن هناك أملأمهما حدث، ولكن ماحدث تخطى كل
حدود الخيال واليقين، قررت أن ترحل لتتركه وحيدا وسط هذاالظلام المدنس، كانت ر
فيقته الدائمة ومصدر طمأنينته وثباته فى أشد معاركه على أرض الخوف، فى أشدالأوق
ات ظلمة وياس وقنوط كانت تنير له طريقه المظلم، كان يطمئن لوجودها كما هى رغ
م علمه وعلمهاأنها لم تعد تعيش معه فى نفس العالم الدنئ، ولكنها كانت صلته الوحيدة
بعالم النور وعالم الحقيقة،كانت تواسيه ويواسيها وقت الشدائد وما أكثر هذة الشدائد ف
ى بلد الموت، لم يكن يبالى بأى شيئ طالماأنها بجانبه ولكن وجب عليه الآن أن يبالى ف
هى راحله، يعلم أنها فعلت ذلك حسرة وألم بعد أن قاتلتوأصرت وصمدت، ولكنه أصب
ح خائفا يترقب غد مظلم لن يستطيع أن يرى فيه سوى الوهم والخراب وهليست بجانب
ه لتدله على الطريق، كما كانت تفعل دائما.وقد حان وقت الرحيل على حين غفلة، كان
يظن أنهاأقوى من تلك اللحظة وأى لحظة، ولكنه لم يتوقع مَكر الزمان ليأخذها منه الآ
ن وهو فى أشد الحاجة لها،عزائه فى أن قلبه كان يعلم أن هذة اللحظة حانت وجاء أجله
ا، وأنها راحلة لتسترىح بعد أن أدت ماعليهابقوة وهدوء وصمت كما كانت دائما..

لم يسمع بخبر جديد إلا أنه تعلم أن حزن الفراق شديد!

Translation:
Yes, she's leaving. He was not being delusional as usual. She could
not bear what she was seeing. She realized that there was a limit to
patience, and its limit lay in seeing her killer bragging and cele-
brating his cruelty and injustice, while everyone hailed and
praised him. She could perceive what they could not. Moaning
and suffering at the decay and death of her dream and the dream
of her sincere comrades in the country of the illusion and the
forbidden.

He was confident, there is hope whatever happens, but what
happened surpassed all limits of his imagination and even his cer-
tainties. She decided to leave him alone amid the sacrilegious darkness. She used to be his constant companion, and his source of
comfort and certainty in his fiercest battles on the terrain of fear. In
his darkest moments, and times of despair and hopelessness, she
would illuminate his dark path. He was comforted by her presence
despite his knowledge that she no longer lived with him in this base

world. She used to be his only connection to the world of lights and truth. They would comfort each other during hard times.

He did not worry about anything as long as she accompanied him, and now he needed to worry, as she was leaving. He knew she did this out of sorrow and pain after she fought, persisted, and resisted, but now he was afraid, while awaiting a dark tomorrow where he wouldn't be able to see anything but illusion and destruction and she, not next to him to show him the way like she used to. Time to leave, suddenly. He believed himself stronger than this moment, but he would never have expected the slyness of time's taking her from him while he needed her that badly. His solace lay in his knowing that the moment had come, and that she needed to rest now that she's fulfilled her duties strongly and calmly.

He never heard any news, but he learned that the sorrow of separations was intense.

But friends didn't relate, of course. They thought I was sad about my girlfriend who was leaving the country or something like that. I wasn't writing it for others, I was just writing because that day I felt I was choking with grief and no one could hear or understand. The pain was still there, but growing more and more, like a cursed embryo come specially from hell feeding on my nervous system through my eye. The medication didn't do anything.

Almost five months of increasingly unbearable pain gnawing my brain, I felt as if they were fifty years. I was taking a lot of painkillers and medicine that couldn't stop it. I wasn't able to sleep, think, talk, hear, or do anything. I lost a huge amount of weight and health. I shut myself away from people, even the closest ones, except for my closest friend, Ahmed.

Many doctors wrote prescriptions without explaining what the underlying reason for so much pain was. Only one doctor doubted something, so he asked to do an MRI and other things, then he concluded that the only way to stop this pain was to eradicate my eye. Because he found that the bullet had been decomposing and was still stuck in the back wall of my eye, so it had been poisoning the eye, and that was the main reason behind the pain and he couldn't intervene with surgery to remove the bullet unless he removed the whole eye! "So, what's next?" we asked, and he replied, "Nothing. It's your decision. When you feel you can't stand the pain anymore come and I will remove it!" I was shocked and relieved; my intuition was right, but I asked if there was any other way besides eradication, "Unfortunately no," he replied. I was resisting removing my poisoned eye with a hope that I might find a solution, or maybe fighting for the last thing that remained from our glorious revolution. But my body couldn't stand my resistance; I was so weak those days. One day I was smoking a cigarette on my balcony as usual, and while I was going back to my bed my whole body fell apart, and in that moment I knew I needed to let it go. Maybe from that day it became so easy for me to let anything go. Even my best friends, my motivations in life, my higher purpose, my belief, even the revolution itself.

But life refused to be done with this dilemma; one of my colleagues at work recommended a doctor to me as I was searching for any hope. The recommended doctor was honored by Mubarak himself; he had put his photos and recognition certificates all over his clinic walls, Ahmed and I were laughing at that, but we said let's see what he can offer. After listening to my story, he said with confidence, "Of course you don't have to eradicate your eye!" We were astonished, "Really!" we replied, smiling. He replied with more confidence, "Do we remove eyes just if they're hurting us?" We replied, "Of course not," almost shouting in our enthusiasm. We cursed all the previous doctors for their ignorance. We get our belief in humanity back because of this doctor who is in the opposite political party but is transcending his bias and is trying to help me! Again, we were so naïve. He was giving me a hard lesson. The operation he proposed was to inject cortisone behind my eye. But it wasn't a cure, it was a curse, it was like boiling oil came direct from hell and poured into my yelling poisoned inflamed eye. Finally, I surrendered and I let it go.

Denial was the headline for the next few months in my life. On the same day as the surgery, with all my weakness and pain from the operation, Ahmed and I went to downtown. My removed eye was still bleeding, but I didn't care. The next day it was very hot, and I went to meet another friend. I thought I was in love with her. But in reality, it wasn't love, it was just a good friendship. But I was insisting, with my empty eye, that I'm in deep love with her. As if I was trying to prove to myself and to the world that nothing happened, I'm still the same.

After one week, I went back to work with my empty eye, just with a cover to protect others from my ugly new face. After one month, I insisted on buying a car! And I did it, with my covered empty eye. I was driving all over town, I'm a normal person and I can love, work, and drive—no, I can drive very fast.

Life insists on teaching me not to be childish or cowardly. The main lesson was that you need to face it, don't run, coward idiot. So after three months of denying what had happened, the first surgery failed, and I have to replace the poisoned empty eye with a device!

The anger starts to rise inside me. What happened? And who is responsible for it? What is this hole in my face? How can I take my revenge? Am I a coward or weak to let that happen without any response? How will I be able to continue my life with that horrible scary face? A lot of questions that couldn't find answers, only anger and aggression were there to reply. From there I started heavy drinking habits and moving away from other people except when I'm drunk. Maybe at that point I found some relief in music, a hard and deep genre in a very loud voice. Dancing alone catching the flow was my only way to release these burning anger flames.

I was refusing to put in the plastic eye (the fake eye). I preferred to live with the truth, the ugly truth, without faking anything. Of course, I surrendered after a lot of fights, negotiations, and talks from family and very close friends. Another wave of rage at the fake face; I really hated my face. I preferred to live with an empty hole rather than fake plastic shit.

By then, I think I was starting to surrender to my grief and sorrow, which opened the hell door of depression. It was like slipping slightly without your consciousness toward hell. I closed my inside doors to life, except for drinking hard and finding escape inside the music. I lost interest in people, in life, in anything. I wrote this paragraph in a private note:

> The permanent status of careening over a thin borderline between a dim light of hope to survive or to release your clinging hands to fall into a deep dark black-hole! His hardest battle was getting up from his bed! Nevertheless, he gets up every day carrying his mountain of grief on his exhausted shoulders, maybe it was influenced by a buried hope that he will, one day, get out of this internal black-hole. He was astonished by people who take life so seriously, especially when they talk about something they found interesting. From where did you get this enthusiasm? He was searching for anything that makes him surprised, searching for anything that can enthuse his bored sad burning soul, observing events going on around him behind a pane of thick frosted glass, screaming in

silence. Living a truly boring life, after a loud interesting busy life during the revolution, wasn't easy for him to continue. What, then? was the only question rolling around in his head.

I was refusing any treatment at this time, which was making me suffer from delusions and start hurting other people, especially the loved ones in my beloved family. I couldn't differentiate between the reality and my delusions; simply I was living in hell and nobody could imagine or understand what was happening. Surprisingly, with all the darkness I was going through, I was inspired with an idea about how to continue our revolutionary goals of empowering people, which turned into a dream, and now it was my full-time job to achieve it!

Finally, I accepted taking medication for my bipolar disorder, and surprisingly, it worked with me. Now I can see the difference between life and hell. I can live without being torn apart between killing myself, destroying the world, escaping from people, or being so excited with a true belief in building a whole new world all by myself in a few days. Without my family's support and care in all my situations, I couldn't make it right now. They helped me to accept what happened, they loved and supported me in many different ways, especially my mother and two brothers. They were the true reason behind starting to love and accept myself again.

Now I have left my job, I'm pursuing my dream with my brothers. I'm recovering now from the past three long hard years. Time was a great mentor to guide me through this tough trip. But finally I can say that I'm transformed from one person to another totally different one. I'm appreciating what happened and I know we still have a long way to see our dream of peace and liberty come true. The main lesson I've learned is that whatever happened to us, we will heal, if we haven't surrendered and keep fighting. And then time will do the rest. Below is what I've written down when I knew that. "She" in the paragraph was my psychiatrist I went to after my second surgery:

Then, she told me: only time will be your friend to heal. I didn't understand her at that time; I was too angry to be able to understand anything. But now, after a hard but true long friendship with time, it seems that she was totally right. Time is so unique; once it has happened, it will never happen again; it became a past, and you will never see it again, except in your memories or dreams. Time is very honest, no matter whether you like it or not; with it you will see the naked truth about yourself, others, and the world around you, even if you were trying to live inside your bubbles of denial or delusions. It will make sure that you have seen them, then it will let you decide your own ways. Time is your wise healer, it will make sure that your wounds are healed, no matter how deep or hard they were, some of them may take more than others, but at the end you will be totally healed.

Time is wise, it leaves scars behind your healed wounds, so that you can remember and never forget your truth. Scars have different tastes of grief, joy, pride, fear, courage, cowardliness, anger, peacefulness, love, and hate.

Time will make sure that you have all of these tastes, with their unique scars deep inside your little heart. I really miss my wise old friend.

Part 2

I still had some remaining questions after I received Kamal's written narrative and asked if he could answer them when he had the time. I asked him for exact dates and events and not to neglect anything that he himself considered vital. He wrote back the next day: "I tried to answer your questions, but it seems that this has opened some deeply buried and painful memories.

I couldn't finish it, honestly, I still remember every second as if
it's happening now, all the small details, pains, voices, different
emotions. I was in deep grief yesterday. I'll try to finish it this
week, though. Sorry my dear for lateness."

I immediately wrote back that he absolutely should not continue and that we would skip the last part. Kamal responded that
it was actually good for him, it was a healing process, and insisted
on writing the last part as well. I think that to reveal Kamal's
pain here is relevant in relation to how we anthropologists work,
obviously in relation to ethics and the responsibility of the
researcher, but also in relation to the difference between when
interlocutors are totally free to select what they would like to say
about an experience and when researchers are posing detailed
questions. Even if Kamal had spontaneously shared these
moments with me before, when they were retold, and maybe as
part of a text, something else happened. Here is the result:

*Would it be possible to add a section about the day when the actual shooting
happened? Or if you prefer, answer the following questions:*

*Exact date, where, and what you did after that? If you immediately under-
stood what happened, what did you feel? Was there a lot of pain? Who helped
you? Did you go to the field hospital close to Tahrir, behind the mosque? Or
what happened? How did they treat you?*

On the 28th of January 2011, in the middle of Tahrir Square, I
was trying to fight back the police forces after they returned at the
head of Qasr El Ainy Street. Before that, they had been defeated
and forced to retreat far away, deep inside this street, so the full
square was under our authority without bullets or tear gas. I can
remember old men and women were moving safely through the
square and taking rest inside the square; the battle had moved
there deep inside this street. We were fighting in groups; after a

long tiring day filled with blood, injured and dead people, killing gas, a lot of bullets and shooting, some groups went to the fighting area and others caught their breath and transferred the dead or injured fighters. But suddenly we all heard a huge scary roar coming behind us from the museum side, it was coming from three huge military tanks, not like the others that were set on fire by us after evacuating their soldiers from them; no, they were really huge tanks. So people, all of them, moved toward the three huge tanks to stop them from entering the square by lying down in front of their treads or climbing on them. After a few minutes I couldn't see the tanks' bodies but I saw a lot of people in the shape of a tank.

At that time the people who were blocking the police forces had come to defend the square from the other side, so the police forces used the opportunity and reorganized themselves at the head of Qasr el Ainy Street again, and started shooting again everywhere hysterically. I can remember old people running from their bullets, then I started to call to people around me that we need to go back to the main battle, it was a moment of panic and chaos for us. I went back with a few of us who recognized what was happening behind. We started throwing stones in their direction, stones were our only weapon besides our insistence on not being defeated by them anymore, we were so close to them we could see them when they were shooting, we turned our backs to them to protect our faces.

Until one of us came to me asking if I can throw stones because he can't and he has gathered some! I didn't reply, of course. I took his stones and returned to what I was doing. At that moment I saw the shooter behind his armor shooting at me or at us, then I heard a crushing sound and felt the bullet crash into my skull's internal bones, it was so fast that I couldn't recognize what happened except from the hell of pain that was coming from my eye, and my whole body, as if I was shocked with a huge electric volt. For a split second I thought it was a killing bullet, but from the pain I recognized I'm still here alive. I didn't shout or cry, which I am proud of, as I faced them, whatever you are going to do we will not be defeated. I touched my eye to understand what had happened, I found liquid with a very small amount of blood, one of us came behind me, took my shoulders, "You are injured?" he asked. "It seems so," I replied quietly. He told me to close my eyes tight, and took me to the field hospital.

At the field hospital that was a few meters away from us I heard a lot of people in real pain, I opened my eye, I saw a lot of bodies, and I couldn't identify if they were dead or alive. My rescue friend moved rapidly to find someone in the hospital who could help me, he came with a doctor, who asked me to open my eye.

Did you go blind immediately after the shooting?

Yes, but I didn't know it then. I knew after about three or four weeks, I can't remember, when I went through the third operation trying to stop the bleeding inside my eye. At that time the doctor told us that my optic nerve had been cut by the bullet and it was still in there but was no danger at all, it would dissolve over time. But I would not be able to see with it anymore.

My Reflection

Kamal's narrative bears witness to how his own body, as well as nonorganic matters such as the bullet left inside his eye socket, the plastic eye (what he called "the fake face"), or the car as a tool of independence and also normalcy, not only create affect but are interlaced with his and others' political struggles, agency and victimhood from the beginning of the uprisings. Further, it is apparent that the damage to his body and its emotional responses, such as denial, rage, depression, loss, and shame follow the time and the rhythm of the political dynamics in Egypt. Kamal does not separate his own body at all from the revolution; he even talked about how it was necessary to sacrifice the eye (or rather that his eye had its own agency) because of his and all revolutionaries' failure in the 2011 revolution.

FUTURITY

Whatever the *experience* of optimism is in particular, then, the *affective* structure of an optimistic attachment involves a sustaining inclination to return to the scene of fantasy that enables you to expect that *this* time, nearness to *this* thing will help you or a world to become different in just the right way. But, again, optimism is cruel when the object/scene that ignites a sense of possibility actually makes it impossible to attain the expansive transformation for which a person or a people risks striving; and, doubly, it is cruel insofar as the very pleasures of being inside a relation have become sustaining regardless of the content of the relation, such that a person or a world finds itself bound to a situation of profound threat that is, at the same time, profoundly confirming. (Berlant 2011, 2)

This chapter took as its point of departure the body and its senses in dense entanglement with living and nonliving things, place, and space and their affective responses to the cityscape, as well as the other way around. We have seen through Kamal's written account how living and nonliving things and affect are working intensely together, where a relation and a flow are created. We have also seen how the notion of the afterlife of the January 25 revolution in 2011 is imperative in order to situate the temporal layer, since every afterlife of a critical event (Das 1995) "influences present-day social practices and creates new affective worlds" (Škrbić, Alempijević, and Potkonjak 2016, 108). New affective worlds are relevant in relation to future as well. The transmission of affect, to use Theresa Brennan's (2004) term again, occurs not only in the present but also extends to tomorrow's children and their offspring. As we all know, our history is an embodied archive that gives knowledge as it transfers lived experiences from body to body. Memory, even when silent, is active. Parents or grandparents, even when they are not communicating traumatic war memories, are able to transfer their affective memories and inscribe them on the bodies of future generations (see Bergson 2007). The sensory experiences that shaped Egyptians' interaction with the world during and after the uprisings will most probably forever be collected in their embodied archive. As the ethnologist Maja Povrzanović Frykman shows with her example of Sarajevo, even twenty years later, her interlocutors' accounts "contain vivid and often gripping descriptions of sensual memories of humanitarian aid—of tastes and smells of food, of clothing items received from distant donors, and of the lingering affective power these things still have today" (Povrzanović Frykman 2016, 79). My argument depends on this understanding that memory exists in the body and need not be conscious to be active in forming people. The body is acted upon by other subjects, by (non-)material matters, and by an un/conscious self. Thus, the body is formed through experiences. As I have argued in earlier work (Malmström 2016), and as the anthropologist Elise R. Johansen points out, "Body memory is something we *are* rather than *have*" (Johansen 2002, 315). A body memory is a "memory that is intrinsic to the body, to its own way of remembering: [it is about] how we remember in and by and through the body" (Casey 1987). Hence, these memories are inscribed in the bodies of Egyptians today, and in the bodies of future generations as well. Acknowledging these body memories of trauma, and that those can be activated and deactivated, and that such memories are present in the bodies of future generations, may help us to better understand the current situation. Moreover, it may also be relevant in relation to understanding "nostalgia for a past future" (Jansen 2016) and to thinking about Egyptian futurity, as an imaginative country that contemplates what will come after (see Muñoz 2009).

TWO

Love of the Motherland and Loss of Its Meaning

Bodies of Passion, Shame, Grief, and Betrayal

LOVE AND INDIFFERENCE

Anthropologist Zakaria Rhani has discussed how affect, materialized as love, was powerfully invested in the Morocco uprisings during 2012, and how love of the self and of the country could be the expression of a political desire. Rhani asserts, "'Love' is not an immutable 'feeling' but, on the contrary, an emergent and contingent experience that unfolds in a particular sociopolitical context and, in turn, shakes the established order of politics. The ethnographic encounter shows that these emerging experiences cannot be scrutinized at the level of discourses only" (Rhani 2013, 12). In turn, the English literature scholar Anke Bartels (2013) raises the example of the Chinese Cultural Revolution, arguing that the conflicting emotions of love and hate should be understood as notions that come to represent the collective passions of a whole nation: love meant love for the country, and hate meant hate

Figure 4. A few hours before President Morsi was ousted, July 3, 2013. Photo by the author.

toward all class enemies, who were viewed as enemies of a progressive China. She shows how passion was used to distinguish between "those who make up the 'us' and those who are 'other' and can thus be legitimately constituted as the object of hate" (Bartels 2013, 43). I assert that love is not the only mode of being during such extraordinary events, and should not be understood as that of being hate's antonym or opposite. Love can also be juxtaposed with other sentiments, such as indifference. It is possible to see a process in Egypt similar to what both Rhani and Bartels depicted in uncertain moments of potential change in "an exceptional time" (Scott 2014, 34), but public affect and its transmission during periods of low intensity, the aftermath of uprisings, and forced moments of stability after such extraordinary political experiences is quite different, as indicated in the introduction. These periods of "the everyday of nothing" are filled with a lack of energy or with shame, rage, grief, and a sense of loss and—most dangerous of all—the lost meaning of the potential new homeland (see Stoler 2008, Gordillo 2014). As the anthropologist David Scott (2014, 21) suggests, both "the alteration in our experience of time, [and] the reorganization of our sense of temporal relation between anticipated futures and remembered pasts" is central for thinking through contemporary matters, as was made explicit in the previous chapter with the narrative of Kamal.

Different Bodies, Different Times

Many of my friends spoke about passion of varying intensity: passionate love during the fervent moments of the uprisings, the "death" of that same love during "slow" periods, and the rebirth of passion (with the same person or another) during new politically intense periods (for more about love, intimacies, and desire in Egypt, see Kreil 2014, 2016a, 2016b; Schielke 2015). Both women and men highlighted certain urban spots, often with dreamy eyes and a touch of nostalgia in their voices. Something similar happened when they talked about the clothes they wore (they were "sacred"), the taste and the scent of the food they ate, and the energy and euphoria they sensed from the crowd in Tahrir Square during the first eighteen days of the 2011 uprisings. A common expression was, "I cannot pass any street corner in downtown Cairo where things have happened without feeling it intensely in my own body." As we will learn more about in this chapter, one object or one place may release an array of affective reactions (see Frykman and Povrzanović Frykman 2016, 18).

But as mentioned above, and in the previous chapter, the aftermath of heated revolts has created other embodied reactions in which depression, sorrow, rage, or painful body memories are common. Even many years later, my friends revealed how they were still "living" in the past: every night reliving the "aggressive hands" of a rape in Tahrir, for example, or avoiding friends or places where it was impossible to cope with the past. Sometimes the agency of the body takes over, as we could see with the example of the "dead revolutionary eye" of Kamal in the previous chapter. The selected narratives in this chapter will let us reflect upon: "Why are 'intensities' experienced unequally, what does it take to 'get' the affective state of the other, and how should we write about it?" (Frykman and Povrzanović Frykman 2016, 18).

FATMA

I have known Fatma for many years. She is an authoritative but also a caring and generous person. Fatma is middle-aged, well educated, a writer, and a divorced mother of two young-adult daughters. We have talked a lot about passion in general and in particular about her passionate relationship over the years with a married man with children, a relationship that started during the first eighteen days of the January 25 revolution of 2011. The periods of high and low intensity between the two of them have followed the rhythm of the political uprisings. It was actually Fatma who made me pay attention to the different waves and to the link between passions between two or more people and uprisings (and she and others introduced me to several "love couples"). She said that as soon as things are "hot," the passions between couples are at their peak, but that they always flag during low-intensity periods: "I really don't know.... I'm quite sure I can't leave him; it's like an addiction, like a circle.... I try to find a way out. When I believe in the revolution again, I start to believe in us again, but when I feel I actually lost the revolution ...."

When I would arrive in Cairo for fieldwork or conferences, the light in her eyes flashed with passion and desire every time she spoke about him or he texted her or when we visited certain locations downtown, but when she showed me photos from the revolution, by contrast, her eyes would glow with rage, fog up with desolation, or fill with tears and nostalgia.

Tahrir Square was their place, she kept saying; every time she was there, she would think of the two of them. Al Azhar Street and the Bab El Louk area were also important for Fatma and so was the tiny vegetable shop near the café she and I often visited. This was the shop where she and her lover had hidden on January 28. The owner had helped them, rolling down the "steel blind," which the police tried without success to shoot through. He also let them use his landline to call her family, since President Mubarak had shut everything down and the cell phones did not work. Fatma talked about her clothes as well in relation to temporalities and frequency:

> I kept all the clothes from the revolution time; I can't throw them away. I have a connection to those pieces. To my love and to the country. Our love relation is the symbol of Egypt; when Egypt is bad, we have bad times as well. Maybe that's why we don't give up; even now, there is no future for us or for [our] country except to keep struggling against injustice, the unfair situation for us and the revolution ... even if we feel hope sometimes, and then give up for a while; but you know ... after a while we feel the invisible power come back to gather us.

How They Met

Fatma gave me the following account about how they met:

> You know, destiny played a big role in our relationship. I met him briefly, Hani, in January 2011, just before the revolution. Around three in the afternoon on January 25, I went to Tahrir Square. Fifteen minutes later, they cut internet and cell functionalities. I was alone in Tahrir and happened to run into some acquaintances. We hugged each other and spent the night together in the square. The day after that was rough, but on January 27, nothing happened. On January 28, I called my father and told him that I had to go out to demonstrate and that I might die, I called my mother and lied, then called my daughters to say a goodbye. I said goodbye to my landlord forever. Then the phones went dead again. I remember that I took a shower because I was maybe going to die that day, and then I prayed. I hurried out of the building, it was like someone told me, "Go out to the street and then you will find him." Outside the building, I met Hani! He did not know where I lived. It was destiny. The same with Hani; he had heard an inner voice telling him to go to my street, and he found me there in front of him.

Weapons, Fear and Airplanes

Fatma remembered during one of our conversations the first time she was totally terrified. This was on January 30, when F-16 military airplanes with their thundering roar accompanied them, repeatedly circling very low over Tahrir Square. Fatma did not want to give me all the painful details, but she realized that she had experienced and seen such terrifying things during those eighteen days that she would never be scared of anything from then on. She had been, she said, in the deepest black hole a human being could be in.

Fatma gave several accounts about running from state bullets, also about Hani's constant protection, but also about the category of apolitical Egyptians, when bullets penetrated the sky. She especially recalled certain moments when they were avoiding being shot. One was when they hid and prayed under the Al Azhar bridge. After about thirty minutes, Hani asked Fatma if she could run, and then tried to. The police shot at them and she fell. Hani helped her. She was shot by pellets. But they made it to join a bigger crowd. "It was completely crazy that day ... so many people, and they built a wall between the two streets with their own bodies." Hani helped Fatma to a poor neighborhood close by to rest for a while. "These men here were not interested. People were dying in the streets, but they were laughing and having their breakfast and coffee.... I remember my rage." Soon they continued to Bab El Louk, where the police again tried to shoot them.

Eros and Thanatos

Late one night, we were sitting on the sofa in my bedroom in our nightgowns, sharing a bottle of wine and talking about life.

We had been talking for hours, as usual, and the vibe in the room was pleasant, safe. Suddenly Fatma began, hesitantly, to tell me about something she never had spoken of before. She kept asking me, "How is it possible?"

On February 2, 2011, the day of the Battle of the Camels, when pro-Mubarak thugs on horses and camels attacked protesters in Tahrir Square (BBC 2012), she was standing with Hani in front of the Egyptian Museum and a young man beside her was shot in the head.

"Maria, he got shot in his brain, nobody knows who did it.... After the 28th there were no police, they did not exist.... Who sent the snipers? ... Nobody knows ... some guys who belong to the police or criminals paid by Mubarak ..."

Someone asked her if she could hold his occiput and she remembered it felt strangely soft. She could touch his brain. It was all over her clothes. The young man died in her arms. At that moment, she sensed a strong, arousing sexual desire. As she recalled this experience, she also told me that this moment was the one time in her life she had ever expressed, by means of words (see Malmström 2016), that she wanted to have sex. She had whispered to Hani (they had met again and continued their relationship), "I want you, *now*."

Fish, Touch, and Harassment

On another occasion, Fatma talked about the day after the day of the Battle of the Camels, when a friend had called her and warned her not to go to the square because the national security personnel and thugs were trying violently to close Tahrir. But she was not afraid, she underscored, and she went with Hani later on. They were hungry, so they went to a local restaurant to buy a large amount of fish, not just for themselves but for others as well, which was what people did during those days. Fatma recalled how they had innocently asked a "spy" for a secure place to enter the square. Suddenly thugs surrounded Fatma, leaving Hani outside the circle, and Fatma shouted something like, "If any one of you animals is thinking about touching me, I will give you hell!" The men tried to grab the food, which she was holding close to her chest, and they touched her breasts and her intimate parts. She slapped one of them, and he hit her back. She fell to the ground. Hani and other men outside the circle tried to help her and at last they managed to get to her. She remembered: "The good guys escorted Hani and me to a safer place in the square. I wanted to go back and hit them with my belt, but Hani stopped me."

The End

Fatma had difficulties talking about when Hani left her for the first time. But once she did. She told me that after the eighteen days, a period in which they had "lived on the streets," where they had been shot at, at least four times (the snipers missed), Hani left her. She did not understand. Fatma began her story with the following words:

"I felt as if my head was being squeezed by a stone, and something heavy was lying on my chest. I had a high pulse, but low pressure."

Fatma did not leave her bed for ten days and she was without food for the whole period. Obviously, she lost a lot of weight. Hani once called one of Fatma's daughters and begged her not to let Fatma slip out of his hands, saying that he would never let her go. But in January 2015, after four years of ups and downs following the dynamics of oppositional politics in Egypt, the relationship between Fatma and Hani was over. She finally left him. His last words were, "You will come back to me." Fatma told me that it would never happen and said with sorrow in her voice: "I will never forget him, even if he has mortally injured me."

The first night I was in Cairo, this time in 2015, she admitted that she had changed, that she no longer had any patience and had a very short temper. During this time, she had been unemployed for a while and had struggled to support her mother and daughters, but was back in a less qualified position at the same workplace. She was frustrated. Tired. It was a total contrast to see Fatma in this state; in periods when she was in love with Hani and with the country, she was eager, energetic, giggling a lot, all the time with dreamy eyes. Now, during this period of low intensity, she kept saying that everything was hopeless; everything was controlled. With time, it was getting even worse. It was as though, during this time, she (and others) did not want to talk explicitly about politics anymore. "You know what's happening" and "You know what's going on" were common phrases of resignation.

My Reflection

Fatma and Hani's passion seems to have followed the rhythm of political waves in Egypt. We can glimpse how specific places and things are connected to the couple's love and encompass their love for Egypt; when, for example, Hani protected her from bullets, they were hiding in spots and dressed in clothes forever linked to the hope for a new country, their political bodies, and their passion. As the ethnologists Jonas Frykman and Maja Frykman describe, "Objects become sensitive through use, but also serve as beholders of affects ... tangibility is crucial for the transmission of affects" (2016, 24). They were in love with each other but also in love with the potentiality of a new nation—strong passion when there was hope in the air and a "dying" passion when it was not possible to grasp any public optimism or activity, the intense responses of these complex forces varying from love to fear, to euphoria, desire, shame, rage, depression, and more.

SALAH

I met Salah only once, through a friend, in January 2014. Of upper-middle age, formerly a businessman in another country in the region, he was a man with a soft, slightly sad, but steadfast, strong visage. We met for one exceptionally concentrated afternoon, evening, and night, going from café to café and then finally to a popular pub downtown. During one moment that night, clenching his hand into a fist, he burst out, "Honesty and love for the country!" And he continued: "Tahrir Square is a holy place for me. Before, I was like everybody else. I lived well outside Egypt, good work, house, car, and money in the bank. But I came home. And I never went back. I totally changed." One of my Egyptian friends had convinced me that I really had to meet this guy, since he had so much to say that would be of interest to me, not least of which was that he had met the love of his life, now his wife, during the 2011 uprisings. The fruit of their passion, a daughter named Thawra (meaning "revolution"), arrived in "the mother of the world" (Cairo) only nine months later.

Salah stressed during that day that all revolutionaries, independent of religious or political affiliation, were united in 2011: "We were one, we thought the same, we did the same." He told me that he had been a leader of one group. He was devastated to experience the increasing polarization during 2014, and he said repeatedly that it was key to stop being an ego. We kept being interrupted by old friends of his at the different places we went to in the course of that afternoon, evening, and night, and they too asked him for his thoughts about the future. He had not met any of them for a long time, avoiding them because he was depressed. He stressed that hope was not gone, but now it was more like 20 percent than the 100 percent it had been back in 2011.

He told me, with longing in his eyes, about all the strong ties he had to people and to the country during earlier times, but he conveyed his present sorrow as well. His eyes filled with tears several times that day, and he confessed that he felt guilty for the deaths of many revolutionaries. It was his fault, he said, because he had asked many to come to the square, and some of them had died there, while he himself was still alive. It was obvious, observing his body language, that one memory in particular was extraordinarily painful. He remembered the moment one of his new friends from the square, who had become as close as his own brother, shouted, "Look out!" and then jumped, taking the bullet meant for him. His friend died instantly, sinking to the ground. Salah said, with shame and guilt in his eyes, that he had been forced to take a step back after the hectic year of 2011 to be able to cope with everyday life. He was not politically active anymore; he was passive.

The Doctor and the Wife

During our meeting that evening Salah told me about how he first met his wife on January 25, 2011, when he was shot in the back with a shotgun. A friend helped him to the field hospital where Lila volunteered as a physician, and Salah told me that the only thing he was thinking about at the time was that he had to get back to the square. Then he slowed down, gave me a roguish look, and said that since their child had arrived in the world only five days after nine months, his friends had joked with him a lot, insisting it must have been all the tear gas, working as an aphrodisiac. Resuming his story, Salah told me that he actually did not see Lila again until they met on February 9, when he went back to thank her for her help. He asked her if she was scared and she responded, "Why should I be?" This was when something between them began to sparkle for him. That she was not afraid to sacrifice everything for her country. "She is not beautiful," Salah emphasized. "It is about respect."

After the eighteen days, some friends invited him to their place, and she was there. Immediately afterward, he told his brother and mother that he wanted to marry, something he had never desired before, and he remembered his brother had asked something like, "What did you say?" and his mother started to cry from happiness. Negotiations took place between their families, they got engaged, and they decided to marry in late November 2011. However, on November 18, the day before the wedding, Salah was back in the square to protest against the military. The demonstration brought together Egyptians from across the political spectrum. Lila accepted and respected that decision since, as he emphasized, "the country comes before everything."

Suddenly he took a deep breath, asked the waiter for another Stella beer, and admitted that they had recently been having a lot of marriage problems. He had told me earlier that he had no employment and that his wife still worked as a physician. He brooded a lot, reflecting, alone, on what went wrong in 2011—alone, because he did not want to have contact with the old revolutionaries. He was too sad, he said.

Salah interrupted himself again and returned to his memories of the henna night (the night before the wedding). He got back from the square around four o'clock in the morning, and when he saw the fifteen hundred prepared sandwiches, he immediately drove back to Tahrir Square with them. His brother called him, asked what he was doing, said that the guests were hungry. Salah replied that his people in the square were also hungry and they were his first priority.

That day and evening and night, Salah told me many, many stories about the experiences he lived through, all of which it would be impossible to recount. He spoke repeatedly about the force, the love he sensed between people during the intense periods of the uprising; and he clearly remembered his emotions in those many intensely lived moments—for example, when he led a huge crowd of revolutionaries toward Falaki Square to fight the state, when he felt not only totally relaxed, but also totally in love.

My Reflection

As we can see, the love story of Salah and his wife is one that has followed the pace of distinct political flows. Something that was notable and explicit is that when I asked Salah for details concerning love, he mixed it with material memories from the more intense days of revolution; everything was woven together. Salah described the couple's passion and their struggle for Egypt as one: the bodies of them and the soil of the nation. The love between Salah and Lila is here an extension of the love for the country. Salah underscored that the love that was flowing between people and the country was the only real power. We can also sense Salah's affective relations with war objects and the cityscape: the tear gas (that was perceived as aphrodisiac), the bullet his friend took instead of him, and how Tahrir Square was transformed into a holy place, where strangers very quickly became a beloved family.

NUUR

Nuur is a creative artist, a politically active, divorced, middle-aged woman without children. She is also a friend, someone whom, from the very first moment of meeting her, I felt I had known for years.

Bodies in the Streets, Bodies from the Past

When I was invited to Nuur's home the first time, she told me that she had assisted in a field hospital based in a private apartment in 2011 close by her apartment and that she could still sense all those dead bodies, not only in the streets but in that home: "Why did all these young people die, at what cost, for what?" She, like Salah, felt deep shame because she had survived. Nuur said, at the end of one evening together, that she, and all the people she knows, no longer have any power, no strength, and that there is no hope for the country.

Nuur talked a lot about her car that she had bought after the uprisings and how she avoided walking downtown: "I need the box between me and the street," she said many times. She drove only to her work or to her family and she seldom met friends, and if she did, it was a totally new crowd far away from downtown. She revealed that to be able to endure any social events in the current moment, she was forced to prepare for days to be able to cope. However, she was still unsure whether the hardship had to do with being able to cope with the everyday, or enduring today's Egypt, or if it was because of everything she still perceived in the invisible.

Nuur was the first person who shared something in the fall of 2016 I had no knowledge about. She (and others I soon realized) continued to experience the past in the present. She revealed that the streets were telling her a story other than the one I could see and experience in Greater Cairo. As soon as she went out of her apartment downtown, she could sense and see dead bodies from the dates of the tumultuous revolts. "The streets are talking to me," she said, and continued, "We see other things in the street. So many layers…"

One afternoon when we met and sipped on hot cinnamon tea, I could suddenly see tears in her eyes, tears I had seen many times before, but this time Nuur remembered one night in 2012 when she was woken up very late in the night by someone screaming outside in the street "O God, only you can see and hear me!" When she looked out her window, she saw a young man surrounded by men in civilian clothes, but clearly from the state security, who were beating him viciously. Three hours later the young man was found next to the garbage in the street, dead. Nuur and others taught me how to recognize these undercover torturers. According to them, these men are physically fit, dressed well but boringly in old-man shirts and suit trousers, clean-shaven, often with a mustache and a *zebibah* [raisin], a mark on the forehead generated by recurring contact of the forehead with the prayer mat. Nuur was silent one moment and she continued, "That's why I avoid downtown as much as possible. But also because of another experience." She hesitated, then recounted a detailed narrative about when she was gang raped in 2011 in Tahrir Square. She hesitantly stated that she had revealed her experiences to only one friend, two weeks earlier, just before she moved to a neighboring country in the region. The past weeks had been extra tough; since then, she is raped in her nightmares every night. "I can sense the same hands doing the same things every night, everything is happening again." The pain in her voice was the pain her body remembered; even if she had tried to forget what happened, every night she was raped again. She was sure she had totally transformed, had aged twenty years since 2011, had changed from a very social to a completely asocial person.

My Reflections

As discussed in the previous chapter regarding body memory, and how we remember in and by and through the body, Nuur's embodied memories may be understood as a repository of the "expression of words in the body" (Brodwin 1994, 95). Nuur's body of pain becomes clearly distinct from the self. In the case under study, bodily agency is expressed foremost through the reliving of pains. In an earlier project about the politics of female genital cutting/circumcision (Malmström 2016), the Egyptian female respondents spoke to me of recurrent pain in their lower abdomen years after the event itself. Some female adolescents told me that without warning, they began experiencing lower abdominal pain when they passed slaughterhouses or when their mothers were cutting meat for lunch. Further, we can also see how revolutionaries are living in different times simultaneously, as with Nuur, who still sees injured and dead bodies from the past in the street, demonstrating the intimate relation between time, bodies, things, space, and place.

TOMORROW WILL BE BETTER?

"Ha, ya Maria, you know that Sisi built another prison. He named it The Future."

(Nuur discussing how she imagined the future of Egypt)

Places and material tools are paths to the world, and as the philosopher Martin Heidegger points out (1996), tools assist us in seeing/feeling the world (Hauge 2016) and any analytics of place should, in my view, "include the affective experience of place-making" (Duff 2010, 893). Since these forces mean a potential that does not have to be realized in language—affect is, as we know, a preconscious experience—it is central to conduct fieldwork in which we, as scholars, stay attuned to the effects of the affect, as Massumi (1995) suggests, since these effects are the only ones that are analyzable. When we use narratives, for example, we must . stay alert also to our respondents' body language: "How affective and emotional layers are connected captures how an interviewee slows down, starts to breathe heavily, sighs and pauses as the narration touches on more demanding topics" (Frykman and Povrzanović Frykman 2016, 16; [see the other essays in the volume *Sensitive Object*s for more concrete examples]).

As became evident to me following the three narratives and all the meetings in Cairo with Fatma, Salah, Nuur, and Kamal in chapter 1, it has been possible to analyze matter, time, place, and space through the prism of the body—the nostalgic body, the hurt body, the raped body, the dead body, and the passionate body. We have been able to follow the gendered political body's love for the country and the state's infliction of violence, rape, and death on the same body; the relational gendered political body and the flow of passion or despair following the waves of time; the gendered political body's ability to live in several times at the same time, where bodies of those killed in the uprisings are still visible to the body of the revolutionary in the streets today. The past and the present are clear and interconnected, but the future is more blurred (see Wool and Livingstone 2017) or is reimagined as lost (Scott 2014).

THREE

Metamorphosing Sonic Rhythm

A Loss of Navigation

POLITICS, BELONGING, AND DISPLACEMENT

I will never forget the sounds of one collective body in Tahrir Square around nine o'clock at night on July 3, 2013, the time and date when President Mohamed Morsi was ousted by the military with support from a large majority of Egyptians. Nor will I forget the street party later and how people were crying, laughing, hugging, or kissing each other. The women and men in downtown Cairo shared an acoustic space of joy. It was a moment of public intimacy. Not far away, however, other spaces had another rhythm, filled instead with people's grief, fear, and rage. The days that followed in the end of that summer were extreme in every sense, and my own body became more incorporated in my field study than I had initially planned. The silence during the pitch-black curfew nights and the sounds of war during the

Figure 5. Downtown Cairo immediately after President Morsi was overthrown, July 3, 2013. Photo by the author.

daytime were embodied, socially shared experiences that have changed the emotional colors of life in Egypt (see also Malmström 2014a).

If we experience affective politics together with our interlocutors through experiencing the sonic materiality of chaos—as I did during the summer of 2013 in Cairo—how can we grasp these affective forces, and what does my selected unit of analysis enable us to say about broader schemes of change or stasis? How does the empirical evidence provide us with conclusive data about changes or the lack thereof at the level of close surroundings? Researchers including historian Ziad Fahmy (2013), anthropologist Charles Hirschkind (2006), musicologists Martin Stokes (2010) and Ian Biddle and Marie Thompson (2013), and philosopher Steve Goodman (2012) have discussed the role of sound in war and revolution,[1] and specifically in relation to transitional North Africa (see, for example, historian Mark LeVine (2008, 2013) and cultural studies scholar Brandon Labelle (2012). As Goodman (2012, 65) put forward: "Sound is often understood as generally having a privileged role in the production and modulation of fear, activating instinctive responses, triggering an evolutionary functional nervousness." Drawing on my fieldwork, I would like to reflect instead on the absence of sound in the floating landscape of Egypt during the summer of 2013, the sound of silence.

In this chapter, affect theory draws attention to how vibrations—being important stimuli within everyday experience as well as having a unique power to induce strong affective states—mediate consciousness, including heightened states of attention and anxiety. Vibrations can both shape and constrain the actions of individuals and groups because vibrations are felt in the body. Consider the sonic materiality of much of popular music: even before you hear the bass, its vibrations call attention to it and invoke an emotional reaction. The vibrations are there, even before they become perceptible to the ears.

AUGUST 14, 2013

My plan for the day was to visit the Rabaa' al-Adawiya sit-in with a male journalist from Al Jazeera. In addition, I had at last established contact with a woman at the sit-in, a young member of the Muslim Brotherhood, who had promised to be my gate-keeper during the day. It was crucial to rely on a gatekeeper to help me conduct interviews and guide me around the protest area. I had been trying to find such a guide for a while.

I did not go to Rabaa' this day, however. During the early morning hours, Leyla, whom we met in the introduction, woke me up to watch the only television in the house, which was located in my bedroom. In an almost exultant voice, she told me, "You are not going to Rabaa' today, ya Maria, it is being cleared out. Let us watch the news!" Dressed in our nightgowns, we began to surf the channels. Some of them were shut down for longer or shorter periods, including Al Jazeera and some of the state-run TV channels' live screenings. This was the first day of horror, when we tried to understand what was going on and what would happen next, nervously straining to comprehend the situation and take control of our feelings about it. Sounds and images from the TV screens, and later from the street and sky outside, affected our senses and shaped our interactions with the world in the moment and, as it turned out, for the future. Biddle and Thompson, inspired by the philosopher Baruch Spinoza, point out that "given that affective powers are relational, insofar as they arise and are modulated by the encounters between bodies, we can never know the full extent of a body's affective powers; what a body might be capable of feeling or doing" (2013, 9). Furthermore, feeling and listening are mediated through various technical devices in our everyday life.[2] The technology of feeling is not intentional; even if we are together with other bodies, it is central first to inquire where are we in that world. As a concrete example, think about screens and speakers and megachurches. People would feel different if the microphones and speaker screens were not there, since in a smaller church people would be able to listen to themselves and to people beside them; that is, megachurches actually create a new body. The speakers in huge churches will produce affect in a certain way, maybe the pastor even becomes divine, and would be a total contrast to the experience of following the same event on TV individually at home.

THE LACK OF SOUND: MID-AUGUST 2013: DAYS OF DANGER

The days after August 14 were extreme in every sense (see Wiemann and Eckstein 2013). According to the *Guardian*, the Egyptian Ministry of Health stopped publishing information on August 17, 2013. A ministry official was quoted as saying that this was "because of the huge number of deaths" (Hauslohner and al-Hourani 2013). Immediately after August 14, downtown Cairo was under military control, and parts of the city became unsafe or impossible to pass through. The violent clashes between Morsi supporters and the army were confined to specific locations, and between those locales one found the streets completely empty, except when people were moving from one place to another. For days, I, like most Egyptians, spent most of my time at home in downtown Cairo. When it was possible, we walked and sensed the surrealistic, empty streets of Cairo before the curfew set in and we were again trapped at home or in someone else's house for the night. Only women were living in the household: Leyla, in her mid-sixties, her adult daughter Shams, a young university student Nadia and her middle-aged aunt Amira, and myself. As a foreigner and a scholar, my position was different; I had alternatives that were markedly different from those of others around me. I could leave the country after a couple of days, which I did at the end of August, after days of being grimly persuaded by my Cairo family (although they could not understand why it took so long for me to return, which I did not do until January 2014). I could seek help from my embassy or move to another area, neither of which Cairenes could do. Further, my earlier life experiences and position were very different indeed from those of my Egyptian friends and acquaintances, which must have affected my experiences of those days. I was extremely ambivalent during this time, partly from shock, partly because of the guilt I felt as I considered leaving the country (a guilt I still bear). Despite these differences, I did notice that some of my responses were shared by those around me. I experienced a body flush with adrenaline—a state I observed in others—which seemed to compel us toward certain kinds of excitements and comforts. Strangely, the chaos seemed to make people more "open," which offered me a unique ethnographic opportunity to explore.

During this period, my own body felt emotionally naked and skinless, and I interpreted my fellows sensing something similar. In odd contrast to the quiet during the nights, during these first days we could hear various kinds of sounds—forces that certainly molded our bodies, senses, and consciousness—such as the shootings outside as well as sirens and low-flying, circling helicopters and military aircrafts. The frequencies a human ear can hear are, as we know, limited to a specific range, but even faint sounds affected and altered us. The scent of anxiety arose from our stressed bodies and from the streets outside and filled the air around us. During these days dramatic changes took hold of the daily rhythms and interactions of the household. The constant need to stay informed was the first need my fellow Cairenes satisfied in the morning and the last one they satisfied before going to sleep; they even sought updates when they woke up during the night. They talked with family and friends about what was happening in their respective areas—in Cairo, in Alexandria, in Suez, and elsewhere around Egypt. We also followed all the news on social media as well as on television. We nervously told each other to stay safe and not take any risks. There were tender, caring, and supportive moments during this space of intense fear (see Winegar's article about affects during the 2011 uprisings). Like many within my Cairene network, I found myself unable to understand my experiences during these early days or imagine what the next day would hold. Despite our attempts to do so, we found ourselves unable to analyze or rationally reflect upon the fluid and violent political situation. We tried to help one another, but we were unable to seize a sense of control from one hour to the next or assuage our fear, confusion, and racing adrenalin. We tried to find security. We wanted to escape. But to where? We were stuck. We sat close together, longing for human touch[3] and relaxation. We constantly went out to the balcony to watch or to listen or to call someone else, longing for some kind of imagined security (see Winegar 2012). Sometimes we fell asleep after a couple of minutes; at other times sleeplessness was very common.

The desire to take control of the situation made us all act strange and do various ill-considered things. There was an explicit longing for sweet treats, especially chocolate, candy, and soft drinks. One day, a member of my household ate so much out of anxiety and stress that she had to throw up during the night. One woman I know living in Alexandria told me over the phone that on August 16 she had gone out, after having been trapped in her home for two days, to buy basic groceries, but she came home with all sorts of sweets and potato chips instead—with no eggs in her bag. Our bodies craved comfort, stillness—the sweet food filled these affective desires, not least (I imagine) because sugar releases the neurotransmitter serotonin, producing a calming effect.

On days we could not go out, the house felt like a prison. It was very scary to be locked inside with the loud sounds of war in our ears. I tried to go out alone as much as possible during the daytime, along with the other household members who were trying to reach their workplaces. Some put in long extra hours so that they could go and return home during safer times. We had to navigate between clashes, away from checkpoints, and around closed parts of the city. Big clashes between demonstrators and the military were not our only concern; there were also several smaller attacks, such as the one against a police station around the corner from our building. With help from my fellows, I soon learned to distinguish among the sounds of the different weapons being used. The day Al-Fath Mosque was cleared, our household could follow what was happening downtown in an exceptional way. I experienced something that was totally new to me: we were watching shootings on television in stereo with shootings from the same violent scene outside our balcony. And the helicopters circled very low over our area—again and again and again.

August 16, 2013, was the day of anger: the day the Muslim Brotherhood asked its supporters to take part in a nationwide Day of Rage after Friday prayers, protesting the forced dispersal of the sit-ins by security forces earlier in the week. We could hear and see on the TV screen in real time how people crossed the 15th of May Bridge from Zamalek toward us, shooting into houses. The brother of a friend's close friend was shot and died instantly when he went out onto the balcony to see what was going on. After that, I thought my friends would stop going out to the balcony, but surprisingly they did not. Neither did I, although I had to flee inside twice as gunfire raged below. Later that day, the Al-Fath Mosque wherein many Muslim Brotherhood supporters had barricaded themselves after the crackdown on the sit-ins, was cleared. Our household listened to and watched the shootings on TV as noise from the same violent scene also entered through our windows. We—a couple of women from different generations and earlier lived experiences—were still completely ignorant of the details of what was going on and what the next step would be. We not only heard and felt, but "smelled" fear in the air, partly from the odor of our anxiety-ridden bodies. The sounds of war terrified us all. In addition to the erratic gunfire from different grades of firearms, we were also bombarded by booming voices through megaphones, sirens, helicopters that circled again and again overhead, and the roar of military jets passing over our heads repeatedly.

To experience Cairo empty, dark, and silent during curfew was a total contrast to every moment of my previous interactions with the city. In sharp contrast to the intense volumes that saturated our days, nighttime introduced a completely different and even more threatening rhythm. The new Cairo was a ghost town. After some nights of the curfew that had enveloped this utterly transformed Cairene landscape, one of our neighbors started to play old classic Egyptian love songs from the 1950s (might be "good to think with" in relation to the 1952 revolution and General Nasser), blasting them at high volume into the otherwise soundless and empty night. It was, in fact, very calming and comforting—the vibrations lightened the mood and made my household companions feel more secure, more connected to the social body of the house. Some members of my household began to sing, and I could see, for the first time in days, that they were smiling. The sound of music gave us a feeling of trust and a sense of belonging. Sound is a language and a knowledge that can bring bodies together (LaBelle 2010). And maybe this was sound as seduction, as Labelle (2010) describes this particular experience of auditory phenomena. It was the sound of a (national) home—but maybe also linked to positive social memories of the 1952 revolution, including earlier military interventions and steadfast love of the country.

Affective politics has this capacity to influence senses of belonging and public intimacy. Despite not being Cairene myself, it was easy to understand this longing for closeness: the collective united body, the sense of home. Hence, the act of listening as our household did during this uncertain period is constantly involved in the production of a sense of home and in mitigating the effects of displacement. Instinctively we understand the sound of violence, aggression, and fear: We run away, take cover, protect ourselves, retaliate. We also intuitively recognize the sound of tranquility and safety. We move through these forces that move through people and produce direct emotional responses as we move through the world. In looking at resonance, vibration, energy, and sound, we are simultaneously profoundly material and intensely ethereal (Malmström, Kapchan, et al. 2015).

Certainly, the affective sonic politics during this intense, fluid period touched us all. Our bodies will always carry the reverberations of these shifting sounds within them; these reverberations have changed us for life. I believe that our bodies will always remember. The silence during the pitch-black curfew nights and the sounds of war became equally embodied, became a socially shared substratum of all subsequent experiences to many Cairenes who lived through these extreme contrasts between day and night, an experience so different from the previous routines of Cairo that they recognized as home. The sound of silence is even more intense than the sound of sounds. The sound of silence is a totally altered rhythm. The sounds of war—shootings, helicopters, shouting voices, sirens—have been part of the soundscape of Egypt since the uprisings of January 2011. The sound of silence, triggered by a decree of the interim government during mid-August 2013, had not been an element of the soundscape in a similar way before. The silence during the curfew in relation to the uprisings in early 2011 was perceived differently. Political opponents to the Mubarak regime recall their sense of a breath of freedom and assurance of a potential better future in relation to the altered sonic rhythm in Cairo. Hence, as ethnomusicologist Ana María Ochoa Gautier notes, "If silence implies a relation between (non) hearing and perception, then it depends on the types of entities or events that produce and perceive it" (2015, 189).

FLOATING

As mentioned earlier, to experience Cairo as empty, pitch-black, and silent during the curfew, something that started in mid-August along with the state of emergency after the bloody turmoil that followed the overthrow of President Mohamad Morsi, was a singular contrast to every moment of my previous interactions with the city. A place I had experienced since the early 2000s was no longer sensorially familiar to me, or to the people with whom I interacted. This was a new urban terrain. This was not Cairo with its familiar busy rhythm, its countless food scents and tastes, crowded Cairo with the loud voice, where it is impossible not to touch one's fellow in the streets. This was a ghost metropolis. It was a move toward something unfamiliar. Everything was floating. It was difficult to orient oneself in the "new" capital of Egypt. We were unable to navigate, not only because of security risks but also because everything had transformed in relation to sight, scent, hearing, touch, and taste. The Cairenes I hung out with during the summer of 2013 expressed it as being "lost in space." But did the silence mute them? It certainly did not, but it did something else.

Performance studies scholar Deborah Kapchan has introduced the term *sound body*, which is defined as a body with multiple rhythms and orientations, and where "[active] listening is a port of entry as well as a method" (2015, 37): "The [porous] sound body is a material body that resonates (with) its environment, creating and conducting affect" (2015, 41, see also Kapchan 2014). She suggests that "if sound is vibration, and vibration is territory, then the sound bodies reorient space and place through their aesthetic practice" (pers. comm.). In the Egyptian context, exactly as "the bird sings to mark its territory," to use Deleuze and Guattari's (1987) vocabulary, the new Egyptian regime created its own territory, changing and controlling bodies through the vibrations of helicopters and aircraft, as well as through the painful touch of tear gas and the sound of silence during curfew. Sounds, or the lack thereof, stimulate, disorient, transform, and control. As Kapchan asserts in relation to her research among Sufis in France, "a sense of belonging is often created through the sonic, which has an intimate relation with the body and with place" (pers. comm.). In a similar way, the various sounds of the uprisings in Egypt have the ability to create a sense of belonging or to inflict a sense of conflict and chaos, instead fostering separations and a sense of alienation, as one can see in today's Egypt. Work by philosopher Steve Goodman is also useful in relation to the new acoustic violence of vibration of Egypt. He discusses fear induced by sound effects, using examples of sonic booms over the Gaza Strip, musical torture in Guantanamo Bay, and the US Army's anticipative strikes in Iraq.[4] He explores the potential sensations of sonic intensity and the moods they provoke among populations. Goodman introduces the concept of "unsound" (not yet audible), but where the unsound still produces neuroaffects; for example, infrasound (27 Hz) was used in the violent French film *Irreversible* to provoke physical reactions. Goodman finds that

> the sonic weapon does more than merely produce anxiety. The intense vibration literally threatens not just the traumatized emotional disposition and physiology of the population, but also the very structure of the built environment. So the term *affect* will be taken in this broadest possible sense to mean the potential of an entity or event to affect or to be affected by another entity or event. From vibes to vibrations, this is a definition that traverses mind and body, subject and object, the living and the nonliving. One way or another, it is vibration, after all, that connects every separate entity in the cosmos, organic and nonorganic. (2012, xiv)

Thus, sonic warfare—or the controlled lack of sonic materiality—is an action of corporeal disciplining (Goodman 2012); the vibrations of military aircraft stimulate, frighten, and control bodies (see Henriques's [2011] analysis of how sound systems operate at auditory, corporeal, and sociocultural frequencies). Precisely as background music can influence people to buy more in the soundscape of capitalism, the hearing of military helicopters or the touch of tear gas may influence citizens to trust (or distrust and surrender to) a new state authority. I believe that the different rhythm of the new soundscape, the absence of sound, does more than sound, something much more dangerous. It produces an ambience of strain and uncertainty. The sound of silence means a loss of navigation, a temporary lapse in orientation. It is important to identify and attend to this vibrational politics of disruption and the affective mobilization of bodies in rhythm as a phenomenon that can be exploited by contesting forces as a form of political violence.

الشرطة العسكرية

FOUR

Vicious Circles of Uncertainty

Vibrant Affective Matter That Matters

As the novelist Marcel Proust once articulated an illuminating phrase about the agential power of things and absences that all of us who have lost someone we loved most certainly recognize. "We think we no longer love the dead because we don't remember them," he said, "but if by chance we come across an old glove we burst into tears" (Proust in De Botton 1998, 156). All the photos on the previous page were taken at Rabaa' al-Adawiya Square one day after the military's clearing of the Rabaa' al-Adawiya and al-Nahda Cairo sit-ins of August 14, 2013, in what Human Rights Watch (2014b) terms one of the world's largest killings of demonstrators in a single day in recent history. The absence of captions for the photos as well as the placement of these images together at the very beginning of this chapter is a conscious theoretical choice, and intimately linked to the very motivation of the text.

This chapter is a collaboration between the photographer and me. The photographer not only shot the photos and composed the captions (see below), she also wrote an account of her experiences in Cairo, especially visiting one of the sit-ins before and after the clearings, linking these experiences to some intense moments at Tahrir Square in 2011 and today's Egypt. The photographer, Thawra (her chosen pseudonym, which means "revolution" in Arabic), is in her thirties, university educated, married, and employed full-time. Thawra participated in the revolts as "an observer in the 25 January revolution, rather than as an activist." She defines the term *observer* as "to be a citizen" who feels so distressed that she wants to experience and document as much as she can "from her own eyes," rather than relying on inter/national media. She attended Tahrir Square from day one, and got involved in a way that "bears no definition." Tahwra recognized an explicit difference between 2011 and 2013 that she wanted to share with me in the beginning of our collaboration:

"Maria," I heard from one of the "new" revolutionists, "Muslim brothers are not humans like us. Therefore, they will get what they deserve." On June 30, 2013, millions of people took the streets; the number was unexpected, and unexpected also was the speed of decisions the army took afterward. In only forty-eight hours, there was an army intervention. In only forty-eight hours, many people accepted "the new president" (Sisi), whom they formally validated a year later. In only forty-eight hours, the Muslim Brotherhood declared they would take revenge and do a coup too. In only forty-eight hours, the dominant national state narrative was that it fought terror, and blood would be spilled, if necessary, in order to defend the nation and defend freedom. A month later, a new wave of patriotism was writing history, but the so-called victory was already "felt," before it happened. On the last Friday of July 2013, I heard some shopkeepers discussing Tahrir as a symbol of freedom and Rabaa' as a symbol of oppression. Buses and cars were parked on Qasr el

Ainy Street, filled with protesters, who began their march toward Tahrir Square with Egyptian flags in their hands. Street cafés had to add more chairs on the pavement and even let guests use the street itself. There was almost a sense of a pilgrimage. During the 2011 uprisings I never experienced such a well-structured form of protesting. Well, it was not the same, at all! It was not the same crowd, the same mood, the same expectations. The same people who wished the revolutionaries to go home or even to be killed in 2011 for the sake of stability and protecting their privileges, the very same ones were the ones who went down the street and demanded justice this day.

The aim of this chapter is twofold. *First*, to explore the clearings of the sit-in dispersals and the political aftermath from the point of view of the materiality of affect, mediated through Thawra, embracing the act of thinking through the things of the sit-ins to reach new insights. It gives attention to materialities themselves, including both the things of the sit-ins, with a focus on Rabaa' al-Adawiya, and the tangible photos—the photos are both indexical, the content of the image, and material, the physical being of the photograph—what I call "thing-materialities," using Bennett's (2010) terminology (for a further elaboration, also about "thing-power," see the introduction). The things mediated by Thawra's gaze and lived experience will be analyzed in relation to different categories of people—thinking-matter, using Hobbes's concept (in Frost 2010)—such as the heterogeneous experiences of those who were and would become part of the field of forces that emanated out of the sit-ins (for example, the Muslim Brotherhood supporters; others who participated in the sit-ins not in support of the Muslim Brotherhood but as an act against the military or in favor of democracy; and relatives, journalists, or observers like Thawra or the military) but also as a reflection in relation to the viewers/ readers of this book. As discussed in the introduction, the post-human turn teaches that the object and observer are not separate and one must take nonhuman bodies seriously (e.g., Ahmed 2006; Leach 2007; Bennett 2010; Braidotti 2010, 2013; Coole and Frost 2010; Goodman 2012; Grosz 2010; Miller 2005). That is also why I use the terms *thing-materialities* and *thinking-matter* in this text. This approach leads to the *second* aim of this chapter, to examine the role of the agential force of both things and humans at the Rabaa' al-Adawiya and al-Nahda sit-ins—to be able to inquire: What will we gain if we shift the focus from human agential uniqueness and add material agency to assist in the analysis of the clearing of the sit-ins and the current dynamics of polarization? If we explore attachment and affinity between people and other materialities at the sit-ins, what relationships with, through, and in the material things will we find (see Purbrick 2014)?

THE FORCES OF PICS

In photography, there is the possibility of communicating, in some way, the essence of a dream, the texture of memory.... Through the alteration, the context of the "memories" (or memory substitute in the case of the photograph, or even, as Barthes described, "counter-memory") there is also the potential for healing, a commemorative process that transcends the personal through the recognition of the human commonalities, there is an intervention, a refocusing and extension of the image meaning.

(Edwards 2014, 122)

In this section I attempt to discuss and reflect upon different affective photo politics (see Barthes 1981; Bergson 1896; Deleuze

1986, 1989; Robins 2014) and why it is so vital to focus on everyday things instead of brutal dramatic scenarios if we would like to grasp a global trauma. In addition, a discussion about what we will gain by thinking through materialities, focusing not only on what is exposed in the pictures in this chapter, things we can see, but also on the presence of absences, reflecting on the power of absences (see Bille, Hastrup, and Flohr 2010). The next section will develop a more empirical discussion, where different examples will be explored of how "materiality is always something more than 'mere' matter: an excess, force, vitality, relationality, or difference that renders matter active, self-creative, productive, unpredictable" (Coole and Frost 2010, 9).

When violent political interventions like the ones at the Rabaa' al-Adawiya and al-Nahda sit-ins take place, the worldwide photo eye is most likely very soon at the scene to cover the human traumas, not because it matters to us all, but because it is breaking news, it is politics, and it will sell. However, the gaze is always on the dramatic and chaotic moments, with a dramaturgical emphasis: fire, smoke, and bodies inflicted with pain or death. This is something onlookers from afar are used to and expect in the representation of such events. By contrast, I am writing against the gaze of voyeurism and the desire to consume human suffering from a remote and safe distance, almost like an action movie. I am also writing against such destructive affective politics. This point is not new, of course. As the writer Susan Sontag (1977), among others, has discussed nonproductive shock and the sense of helplessness and blunting of emotional response the more the vision is exposed to spectacular affective images of pain and conflict. The global mainstream media, with a certain political and economic agenda, seldom has time, or interest, to employ an alternative political approach or to follow up and explore the everyday lives of people after a tragedy. This arrogance leads, through the materiality of affect mediated via sensationalist photos, to the production of specific sentiments, which, in my view, is not fruitful for a deeper understanding, and is even dangerous for the global political body. But there are exceptions to conventional conflict photography—photographs that depict survivors a long time after the trauma, which may even exclude images of human beings.

In the spring of 2015, when I had written the first draft of this chapter, I came across a beautiful article written by the *New York Times Magazine* essayist and photographer Teju Cole. He presented several examples of alternative photo work, by Sergei Ilnitsky, Vasily Fedosenko, Glenna Gordon, Sam Abell, and Gilles Peress, and one photo/grapher especially communicated intimately with my work:

> In Ilnitsky's photograph, taken last August in Donetsk, a major city in the eastern part of Ukraine, a length of white lace is swept to the left side. Like a theatrical curtain, it reveals a table with a teapot, a bowl full of tomatoes, a can, two mugs, and two paring knives on a little cutting board. It is a still life, but it is in utter disarray. Broken glass and dust are everywhere, and one of the mugs is shattered; to the right, across the lace curtain, the shards of glass and the table, is a splatter of red color that could only be one thing. Domestic objects imply use, and Ilnitsky's photograph pulls our minds toward the now lost tranquility of the people who owned these items. How many cups of coffee were made in that kitchen? Who bought those tomatoes? Were there children in this household who did their homework on this table? Whose blood is that? (Cole 2015, 23; see references for the link to the photos)

Ilnitsky's photography transmits a bloody interruption of the stillness of habit, shocked into life by its very absence, the sound of silence after the crash. If—as the photographs in this chapter, like those by Ilnitsky, demonstrate—crises are presented through things, including the very absence of people, then this move, I assert, makes room for reflection and the possibility of a slower pace. Things, the leftovers, witness the past, but they are also intimately linked to the present and to the future.

How the images in this chapter will affect the viewer is obviously also dependent on how much background knowledge the person has. There is a vast difference in the forces of affect among different categories of people; for example, between and among scholars who analyze the trauma shown in this chapter, relatives of those who died at the sit-ins, Egyptians who perceive all members of the Muslim Brotherhood as terrorists, or the military, who were commanded by the interim state to clear out the sit-ins. Further, there will be a difference depending on whether the viewer looks at the images alone or with others. The affect will differ and will constantly flow for persons over time and through different contexts (see Pinney 2005). As the scholar and artist Christina Edwards put forward: "The image may appear to be the same, but the interpretation and response to the photograph will be different, as the viewer in the present has altered with time. In the repeated viewing of a family photograph, other memories become interlinked with the original image" (2014, 113). Hence, who the viewer is, temporality, and context are significant variables that must be included in the analysis. However, what we will always gain using the lens of the materiality of affect is that, once manifested in the physical world, otherwise vaporous and fleeting sentiments become graspable, at the level of everyday life as well as academic enquiry. But then again, there will always be a fluidity in the forces of affect (figuratively and literally at one and the same time).

In relation to the viewers of the photos of this chapter, I would like, on the one hand, to discuss the many filters there are from the very beginning; for example, the interpretation and selection of others' interpretations and choices. Thawra and I have already selected the photos used in this chapter and these are selected and shot through Thawra's gaze. Only three of our selected six photos were accepted by University of California Press, since three images were not of print quality. On the other hand, all the things left behind and exposed by these photos will most certainly lead to a different materiality of affect than the photos of the mainstream media. Through the process of thinking through things, it may be possible to experience the absence, the traces of the lived bodies' everyday life and the remains of the Egyptian bodies at the sit-ins, at a calm pace, in a way that is possible for the viewer to digest. As the archaeologist Severin Fowles points out, "Absences perform labor, frequently intensifying our emotional or cognitive engagement with that which is manifestly not present" (2010, 27).

In a totally different context, as the anthropologist Rebecca Empson (2007) elaborating on kin relations in Mongolia explains that the making of kinship is achieved through the separation of bodies and that people manifest themselves via things; for example, they are able to be in many different places at the same time. Hence, I assert that relations are created between the viewer, the things, and the absent bodies through the *doing* of these particular photos (see Empson 2007). Hence, the everyday things that we can grasp from the action of viewing the photos leads to a transmission of affect via the things, and the viewers uncover simultaneously the owners of the materialities. In exploring the objects–subjects relation in the particular context of Egypt, we will learn something new from the perspective, I propose. My main argument here is that if we take thinking-matter and thing-materialities seriously, we will have two new innovative analytical tools, as Bennett, drawing on a Spinozist notion of affect, suggests: "the first toward the humans who *feel* enchanted and whose agentic capacities may be thereby strengthened, and the second toward the agency of things that *produce* (helpful, harmful) effects in human and other bodies" (Bennett 2010, xii). At this point, I would like the reader to experience the photos again, but this time with the photo captions; most probably, there will be an alteration in experiencing the images together with the captions written by Thawra. But first, I would like to include the captions of the three remaining photos (the ones that were not printable), since these photos are also valuable for our argument. The first one showed a protester's toothbrush on top of a poster of Mohamed Morsi. The second image exposed a burnt prayer rug draped over a fence, and far behind, a military policeman who guards the area of the sit-in dispersed the day before. The last photo is a satellite dish penetrated by bullets.

Do the things mediated via the photos reflect intentions of the absent bodies or/and do they independently expose qualities of their own? Are the things exposed in the photo's extensions of particular persons, the collective of the sit-ins, of relatives and families, of the global Ummah, or of all? As Cole rightfully states, "Objects are reservoirs of specific personal experience, filled with the hours of some person's life. They have been touched, or worn through use. They have frayed, or been placed just so" (Cole 2015, 24).

MATTER THAT MATTERS

Objects have the longest memories of all; beneath their stillness they are alive with the terrors they have witnessed.
(Cole 2015, 22)

Figure 6. A broken mirror, an eyeglass case, a single shoe. Rabaa' al-Adawiya Square, August 15, 2013. Courtesy of an anonymous photographer.

Figure 7. A *taqiya* (Muslim cap) wrapped on a wooden railing surrounding a former green space that became a burned-out enclosure of sand after the dispersal. Rabaa' al-Adawiya Square, August 15, 2013. Courtesy of an anonymous photographer.

Figure 8. A shield, with the text "Military Police." In the background, prayer mats lie outside the mosque, where the bodies of dead protesters were gathered for identification. Rabaa' al-Adawiya Square, August 15, 2013. Courtesy of an anonymous photographer.

Let us now move deeper into the scene, closely imagining the urban landscape of Cairo during the late summer of 2013, especially the sit-in of Rabaa', with the help of the photos but also mediated by Thawra's lived experiences, a slightly different angle since it is a narrative written by Thawra, the photographer. Again, because of the aim of this chapter it is a conscious choice not to analyze Thawra's account in this section. Thawra's account is another layer of language, and the transmission of affect here will be dissimilar to experiencing the photos alone.

Thawra's Story (Spring 2015)

August 15, 2013. In the morning after the dispersal, all sorts of burnt things and dark and heavy dust covered the two roads of

Rabaa' (not even a dog would go and try to find anything to eat among the burnt bushes). The smell of tear gas was still perceptible, and there were bullet holes in virtually all the buildings. Two months of sit-ins had abruptly come to an end. The dead bodies were gathered in the nearby mosque, where the families were forced to queue to identify their relatives under the close surveillance of Military Police. I wondered as I walked around how the protesters who had not been killed could find their way out during the clearing of the sit-in. The artifacts left behind were mainly daily-life things such as toothbrushes, shoes, prayer carpets, and shirts. All sorts of things that describe a family's daily life, stuff from a home, and certainly not leftovers of professional terrorists as was and still is repeated in the dominant national narrative. I started to take pictures of these things. Shooting photos of these artifacts aims to build up an archive that says what the News cannot express. It allows me to recall details from the past events that the mainstream media deprive us of (which erase personal things and emotions). The photos of the things at Rabaa' prevent me from forgetting all the humans who died. The few who wandered around this day looked as if they were dazed. Their only gaze was focused on the ground, where they sometimes picked up an item. I saw one man, for example, who gathered shirts left behind. Was he a protester, relative, or a scavenger? I simply could not ask him. The cleaning campaign was already active with bulldozers, carting away what it deemed junk and wastes.

Remembering April 9, 2011. Strangely, there was no blood at Rabaa'. The absence of blood was striking, but the death toll as well as the bodies in the mosque proved a massacre. I expected to see blood stains as part of the colors of a massacre, partly because of another massacre I had witnessed after it happened, on April 9, 2011, where blood was everywhere the morning after. What I had in my thoughts was the night of April 8, 2011, when commandos approached Tahrir Square. Trustworthy sources, who had joined the sit-in for the night—which I did not, for reasons I will describe below—gave me a story that differed from the fabricated ones we read afterward in national media. I was monitored by some military officers as I went back and forth between my apartment and the square during the day, and they arrested me for a short while. I had been arrested by the same officers two months before, and we actually recognized each other. The arrest gave me the sense that a violent dispersal was probably going to happen, especially with the presence of face-masked men from special commando units around Tahrir. I decided that it would be too dangerous for me to be there at night with fewer people on the streets. The morning after, however, a friend called me and asked me to come as soon as I could and to bring my camera. It was already around eleven o'clock when I arrived at the square. I remember that the sky was invisible, and the sandy wind swept dust and broken pieces of barbed wire over the place. A small group of protesters stood on the central platform of the square and gave their testimonies to the very few who passed by. At one corner, in the middle of piles of garbage, and close to one of the green railings that fenced the square, a man pointed with his finger to ... the remains of human flesh. It was like the body parts yelled out the story of the massacre. I heard that the rest of the bodies had been taken right away by the commandos. I do not know if dead or alive.... At that moment I was the only one with a camera around, a few joined thereafter, but there were no official media professionals. What I witnessed was not broadcast on national TV. I think even now only a few dozen people in Egypt—surviving victims, perpetrators, or witnesses—know and remember the bloody details of that massacre. That day, I came back home with my camera full of pictures. I fought against nausea, and against a feeling of guilt. I tried to figure out what they were for: to tell a story that would only be taken for another false story? Anyone who tried to expose the untold, as an Egyptian, as an accredited journalist, or as a victim, found themselves banging their heads against unhearing walls.... No one would listen to them....

The day of the massacre, August 14, 2013. A bloody battle that would change our way to look at each other was about to happen. A friend came home to me in the afternoon, hours before the dispersal of the sit-ins early the next morning. He actually had a nervous breakdown, where among other things he shouted out, "A genocide is going to take place and no one does anything to prevent it from happening!" We stayed silent because there was nothing else to do. Night came. I could not sleep the night before. At six in the morning. I heard loud sounds. I looked out of the window and gazed at my neighbors on the rooftop right in front of my balcony. They were watching TV. I immediately realized a massacre was on. And yes, afterward, it was too dangerous to speak about. If you did, you would have been taken for a Muslim Brotherhood sympathizer or member. A witch hunt was and is still ongoing.

The sit-ins before the dispersals. One dominant narrative during the time just before the dispersals was that people at the sit-ins gathered weapons and prepared themselves to invade Cairo city, and maybe the whole country as well. Another narrative was the one of a peaceful sit-in. I wanted to visit one of the sit-ins to experience one other than Tahrir, which was led by many of the same people who took part in the sit-in of January 25, 2011, but who thereafter betrayed it. They came back with a new leader, a new dictator, and only accepted their own views in the making of the new Egypt. But were they the only ones who tried to enforce their grand plan to the rest of the nation? Not at all.... The Rabaa' and al-Nahda (I did not visit al-Nahda, because it was closed by the army at a very early stage) sit-ins were not located in the heart of downtown Cairo like Tahrir, but more like hidden in a corner ... far from most eyes ... far from everything, especially the one in Rabaa'. However, the Rabaa' sit-in was everywhere on the news. Anti-coup channels as much as Muslim Brotherhood channels broadcast the sit-ins, but there were fewer broadcasts from al-Nahda. In fact, you were able to sit in front of your TV and follow the square day and night: you could eat and sleep at Rabaa', listen to the speeches held there, and pray with the prayers there, in front of Rabaa' Mosque. During the summer of 2013, Rabaa' was open for visitors, such as foreign journalists, and tours were offered, even in English, if needed. The landscape at the Rabaa' sit-in was very different from Tahrir Square. If Tahrir exposed protesters to the danger of too many entrances, where the riot police or thugs easily could find their way in, it also had many exits for protesters to escape through, instead of being a rat in a cage waiting to be killed, as was the situation at Rabaa'. The Rabaa' sit-in looked like a village, where you could find all the everyday necessities, for example, TVs, satellite dishes, food carts, and even a souq (market). In one of the two long avenues it was possible to buy clothes, camping chairs, and many other things. There was a great solidarity, and everything was very well organized. At the same time, I sensed an extreme fragility and a fright, explicitly shown in the people's faces, but also in their words and gestures. At each end of the avenues, groups of men wearing motorcycle helmets and armed with sticks rehearsed. It did not look like a professional military unit, but one based on a great fear of being attacked. It was possible to feel in the air that Rabaa' was a bomb about to explode.

Trying to cope with today. The city of Cairo woke up with a bitter taste in the mouth (August 14, 2013). And thereafter ... trying to continue life ... I tried to explain to my friends and acquaintances (many of whom I would lose after the summer of 2013) why I did not celebrate a massacre, why there is no victory to be proud of, why I could not breathe anymore, because of killing in the name of the state, with so much blood, and old-new psychological terror on everyone. Back to the old time, before 2011, talking was dangerous again. It was summer, but when I remember that period, I feel cold, so cold. After the summer of 2013 I changed. A long period has passed and I still feel anxiety every day. I even started to talk to myself at that time, and I still do. It took me a year to acknowledge I had a trauma, to realize, somehow, all the gas I breathed, all the blood I saw, all the screams I heard, and all the arrests that were made during the 2011 uprising.... But I could not comprehend the 2013 silent terror. From that moment, I did not experience so much violence directly, just sensed the aftermath of viciousness. There I experienced trauma. I was totally alone at home in silence during the beginning of the curfew. If we compare 2013 with what we experienced during 2011 ... the only thing left today is to watch propaganda from TV and radio at home and get disgusted, or write alone, or dream alone. I know that nothing would change if not shared collectively. An open public space, such as Tahrir, allowed exchanges of ideas and unavoidable disputes—necessary for a society not to go back to sleep. It is better to share disagreements rather than, as we do today, remain mute and frustrated. The latter disposition has led us to become a more depressed and disillusioned society than ever. Getting trapped into nostalgia is dangerous. However, a number of initiatives, like theatre plays, grow as hidden protest (otherwise you will be jailed; you can be critical in poetry if you use symbols and do not speak directly . . .) against the current regime.

For over a year, while walking on the streets of Cairo, I often wondered if I encountered any of those who managed to escape from the dispersals. The thoughts in my head were: Did they fly away with all the blood? Only leaving behind the few daily items that marked life? Today I try to ignore the ghosts and relearn how to walk free of my pervasive anxiety.

MATERIALITIES AT RABAA' AL-ADAWIYA

We need to delink pain from the quest for meaning and move beyond, to the next stage. That is the transformation of negative into positive passions. . . . This requires a double shift. First, the affect itself moves from the frozen or reactive effect of pain to the proactive affirmation of its generative potential. Second, the line of questioning also shifts from the quest for the origin or source to a process of elaboration of the questions that express and enhance a subject's capacity to achieve freedom through the understanding of its limits. . . . The ethical process of transforming negative into positive passions introduces time and motion into the frozen enclosure of seething pain. It is a postsecularist gesture of affirmation of hope, in the sense of creating the conditions for endurance and hence for a sustainable future.

(Braidotti 2010, 214)

My inquiry here and now is: How did these thing-materialities and thinking-matter affect not only the observers of these events and the relatives of those killed, but the military, the journalists, and the voyeurs in the days after the dispersal and onward, and how did these heterogenic categories affect each other and the other materialities? The everyday items for the people who lived here during the summer of 2013 transformed immediately into garbage, as matter out place, to use Mary Douglas's (1966) classic term, precisely like the deceased people. As we can see, there is no separation between the nonorganic and the organic materialities. We as viewers, if not at the sit-ins then via the photos, may also grasp that these everyday things are not only intimately linked to but part of the absent bodies. The place(s) where these things are kept afterward is equally important. The transformation of the identity of things into trash was, I assert, a necessary manifestation for the state clearing out matter out of place (specifically, thinking-matter as well as other thing-materialities). Hence, the unwanted marking of these bodies as strange, not authentic, and as matter out of place, was, in my view, a necessity for the state to be able to eradicate so many unwanted Egyptian bodies at once within such a short period of time. These once-lived bodies, as well as the wounded ones, were transformed into something more than garbage, to something else. They became "the others" on multiple levels. In Egypt, the slogan "war on terrorism" immediately became the national refrain of both the state and private media on August 14, 2013, and it is still dominant within the national rhetoric. In order to eliminate certain Egyptians bodies that had suddenly developed into things/bodies outside of national belonging, space, and place, they first had to be produced (see Wilcox 2015a). These political bodies were made, by the Egyptian authorities, into the bodies of terrorists/non humans.

I have written elsewhere (Malmström 2014e, 2015a), in relation to suicide bombers in Palestine, where I draw on the anthropologist Natalia Linos's (2010) insights about political bodies, that these men reclaim the physical Palestinian space through actions of self-destruction, by the help of the "polluting" power of their bodies. At Rabaa' al-Adawiya, even if no bodies were left, the power of the absent political bodies was still there via the things. If we think about the everyday artifacts left behind in the photos as an extension of the absent bodies, and not simply as the military's disruption of the order of things in the liminal home of the sit-in protesters and the protesters' habitual ways of being in the world (Bourdieu 1977), we can see that these materialities "stand for relations that are reflected through the gaze and interpretations of others" (Empson 2007, 134). Secondly, if we think about the thing-materialities at the sit-in, where the viewers of the photos, as well as the actors who actually were at the very spot, gaze at a sandal, or a prayer mat, there are simultaneously materialities that the viewer will not be able to see, but they still acted. Vibrant matter, to use Bennett's (2010) concept again—body fluids such as blood on the ground, skin cells on a towel, or dried saliva on a toothbrush—all these memory-things were there; they acted, and they affected the ones who experienced the sit-in. The bio-aspect of agency here—such as various assemblages of microorganisms, hair, or fingerprints—even if not seen, was still part of the things at the sit-in. Hence, the scent of war on worn garments, for example, or wounded and dead bodies that leak into and onto materialities, and the sensory experience of handling these destroyed everyday things and bodies, all act upon the bodies who were there. Thinking through thinking-matter and thing-materialities teaches us, among other things, that our bodies also are other than ourselves, since we consist of different materialities, and other live matter lives inside and outside of our bodies.

Bennett's enchanted materialism encompasses (in)organic things as agential actors that challenge human will, and here is a concrete example of that. But how these acts influence the future we do not yet know. What we know is that these lively materialities, with their agentic capacities (Coole 2010), and their affective presence (Armstrong 1981), literally embody the absent bodies. This absence can be used to heal; it can be an agential force, but it can also be destructive. I will give a few examples, starting with Thawra and her photos, where the presence of absence, and therefore the very presence of the dead bodies, suggests the following: First of all, shooting the photos of the different thing-materialities at the sit-in is Thawra's agential act to make the state massacre understandable and to make the surreal real. As Thawra writes from another scenario in 2011: "Anyone who tried to expose the untold, as an Egyptian, as an accredited journalist, or as a victim, found themselves banging their heads against unhearing walls." That said, absences perform labor (Fowles 2010), as described above. Furthermore, Thawra was, by sensing and shooting everyday things linked and part of the deceased, able to experience the power of the absent bodies and, as she writes, "to build up an archive that says what the News cannot express. It allows me to recall details from the past events that the mainstream media deprive us of (which erase personal things and emotions). The photos of the things at Rabaa' prevent me from forgetting all the humans who died." By taking the photos, Thawra was also able to communicate the textures of her painful memories and to deal with feelings of guilt and anxiety. The photos are obviously part of a therapeutic process, and as Edwards writes: a "potential for healing, a commemorative process that transcends the personal through the recognition of the human commonalities, there is an intervention, a refocusing and extension of the image meaning" (2014, 122). In the end, aspects of temporality and frequency are also central here. The massacre in 2013, but also the state control, the silence, and the abstract violence, as well as the difficulty to grasp what has happened and what Thawra defined as "the 2013 silent terror" exposed earlier lived experiences from 2011. As she writes: "I had a trauma, to realize.... Somehow, all the gas I breathed, all the blood I saw, all the screams I heard, and all the arrests that were made during the 2011 uprising never generated trauma ... but I could not comprehend the 2013 silent terror. From that moment, I did not experience so much violence directly, just sensed the aftermath of viciousness. There I experienced trauma."

Although I have not talked to all the other categories of people who visited the sites, I will give some thoughts about their potential emotions, transformations, and agential actions: The relatives of the absent deceased who recognized things at the site most probably sensed some comfort bringing these material embodiments of love home (see Moran and O'Brien 2014, Purbrick 2014). Hence, in the desire for something irrecoverable, the materialities from the sit-in might be employed to reconnect with beloved bodies, things that at the same time represent memory, love, and loss. As the historian Leora Auslander notes, "People never really outgrow their need to incarnate in objects those they love" (2005, 1019). Furthermore, absence may be used in the future as a powerful political agential tool against the state, something the anthropologist and archaeologist Zoe Crossland (2002) shows us in her work on the disappeared in Argentina, where relatives transformed the trauma of absence from negative to a positive in their protests against the regime. (For a discussion about absent bodies of political violence, categorization, and ambivalent exhumations, see also the anthropologist Layla Renshaw's [2010] example of Spain.) Finally, and what I find is vital to understand what happened in Cairo in 2013 in relation to now: the bodies of the Muslim Brotherhood supporters are transformed into visible objects of the state, but remain invisible as social beings (Amar 2013).

THE ABSENCE OF AMOR FATI

> I want to learn more and more to see as beautiful
> what is necessary in things; then I shall be one of
> those who make things beautiful. *Amor fati*: let that be
> my love henceforth! I do not want to wage war against
> what is ugly. I do not want to accuse; I do not even
> want to accuse those who accuse. Looking away shall
> be my only negation. And all in all and on the whole:
> some day I wish to be only a Yes-sayer.
>
> (Nietzsche 1997, 148)

It is to be hoped that the viewer/reader of this chapter is able to "touch" (and be touched by) those now lost to touch via materialities in a way that would not been possible through the gaze of voyeurism and is now open to further thoughts and reflections (see Barthes 1981, Hsu 2000). I would like to highlight the following: If we recognize all things (organic and nonorganic) as inseparable, although some materialities, like people, are more of thinking-matter, we will gain an alternate and an innovative understanding of what happened during this national day of trauma as well as its aftermath. Thinking through material aspects of public affect lets us think about power relations in a specific way. The discourses that produce certain subjects as inhuman, as justifiably killable, through subjectivity, are a material engagement in the world (see Wilcox 2015a). After the clearing of the sit-ins, the regime immediately moved away bodies and things. I assert that the thinking-matter and thing-materialities are, as mentioned earlier, an example of what

Douglas (1966) means by human waste, as matter out of place, as dirt and shame. Impurity implies disorder, and order must therefore be symbolically re-created. As Douglas so rightfully contends, "Ideas about separating, purifying, demarcating and punishing transgressions have as their main function to impose system on an inherently untidy experience. It is only by exaggerating the difference between within and without, about and below, male and female, with and against, that a semblance of order is created" (1966, 4; see also the philosopher Julia Kristeva [1982] about clean and proper bodies).

If immateriality can be expressed only through materiality, as the anthropologist Daniel Miller (2005) argues, then in Egypt politics and religion were merged into a specific version of political Islam that had to be eliminated in order to save the country. The Muslim Brotherhood and their belonging to the global Ummah actually threatened the national borders. They became suspicious, deviant, dangerous bodies that do not fit with the boundedness of the state but must be excluded in order to protect the clean bodies of proper Egyptians (see Wilcox 2015a, 2015b). The political bodies of the sit-ins became embodied into bodies, without subjectivities, whereas the state actors simultaneously became immaterial and disembodied, since their bodies were not subject to violence (see Wilcox 2015a, 2015b). Hence, the materiality of affect is significant in the making of the other under the umbrella of nationalism.

GRAND NARRATIVES OF RABAA' AL-ADAWIYA AND AL-NAHDA

Grand narratives about massacres almost always entail a will to power between and among interpretations. Interpretive variants depend, to a large degree, on different ideological roots; in the case at hand, between two institutions with two narratives of Egypt's history and future: the modern nationalist movement, on the one hand, and the revivalist Islamist current, on the other. Both narratives are engaged in the manipulation of consciousness. Who has the right to speak on behalf of history? Who has the right to exist?

Following Hobbes's thoughts on imagination in relation to the grip of national posttraumatic stress disorder in Egypt, where he suggests that "imagination is a form of memory that comprises past perceptual experience, past affective responses, as well as current perceptual and physiological stimuli," we can further understand why Egyptians were, in the political landscape following the massacre, afraid of their own imaginations, particularly imposed by the forces of affect—of a created enemy (see Frost 2010), as we learn more about in the next chapter. I assert that what I term the "national collective body of trauma" developed quickly during these first days of horror (especially in combination with the extraordinarily affective lived experiences among Egyptians since the January 25 revolution). What I find of particular interest in relation to the dynamics of polarization in Egypt is the temporality of fear in relation to the imagined control and safety—that is to say, "how the movements of memory and anticipation in fear place the subject in relationship to time in such a way as to give her a sense of possible mastery over the field of her actions and (therefore) over the future" (Frost 2010, 165). In other words, the temporal movements of fear enable the subject to imagine herself as an effective agent (Frost 2010, 169).

FIVE

The National Prison of Politics

Masculinities, Nationalism, and Islam

This book has dealt with both the backstage and the frontstage of politics in Egypt, especially since the 2013 takeover by the military, through connecting two bodies of theory—affect and materiality. I have tried to bring "large-scale events such as war, public demonstrations, state-sponsored violence and armed repression into the scale of the everyday, the bodily, the sensory and the local" as well as to bring the "backstage and the frontstage of politics into a deep dialogue."[1] This chapter is an attempt to recapitulate the elements presented in this book in order to give a coherent analysis of the situation in Egypt today and the eventual imaginations of tomorrow—focusing on the body of change and adding some new layers of analysis to its object—as well as to make explicit the relevance of my theoretical approach.

Figure 9. A closed elevator and entrance to a popular downtown bar. Photo by the author.

A "REAL MAN," WHILE EGYPT FALLS APART

After the military's repression and forceful dispersal of the Rabaa' and al-Nahda sit-ins in the early morning of August 14, 2013, General Abdel Fattah Saeed Hussein Khalil el-Sisi (who was appointed first deputy prime minister while remaining minister of defense after President Mohamed Morsi was ousted on July 3, 2013) spoke to the nation on national television about the need to fight terrorism. I had known Leyla, whom we met in the introduction and chapter 3, and her household since 2002 and considered them all to be analytical and politically aware. Suddenly the living room and bedroom seemed suffused with a thick sense of nationalism; the household members offered no criticism or reflection. But the mood of the family was not about nationalism alone. It was also a sexualization and a gendering of Sisi into the figure of the patriarch, a common depiction of hegemonic masculinity embodied by earlier Egyptian military-political leaders. The women of my household said that Sisi was someone special—he was very sexy. Another female friend, Nuura, told me in mid-August that many of her male journalist colleagues had told her, in a joking way, that they felt "bad" because all Egyptian women were suddenly abuzz about how masculine, sexy, and handsome Sisi was, and they could not compete. When I asked Leyla what she thought, she said she was way too old, but then she giggled and agreed that he was a man with good manners and style, and someone that Egypt urgently needed. She also said that although she certainly had not liked Mubarak's politics—and had been in the square protesting against him—he too had both class and manners. The Cairo residents I associated with during the summer of 2013 recognized Sisi as "a real man" whom they could trust, in contrast to the deposed Morsi, who was perceived as weak, stupid, unmanly, and devoid of manners and class. What had happened? What was this all about?

SISI FEVER: EVOKING THE TASTE OF HOME

There are countless examples of materialized experiences consciously constructed by the current autocratic military regime, as we have followed throughout this book, that have evoked passionate affects among Egyptians since the *Thawret 25 yanāyir* (January 25 revolution); these materialized experiences are also connected to how gender is produced, reproduced, unmade, expressed, and negotiated (where my focus is on floating masculinities).[2] Further along, this point will be illustrated with ethnographic examples drawn from my own observations (a few of which were described in earlier chapters) and those of others; for now, however, allow me to mention several notable examples: the sharp contrasts between the whir of a military helicopter versus the strange silence of an empty Cairo street during the summer of 2013 (marked contrasts from day to night as described in chapter 3); the appropriation and commodification of revolutionary symbols, as the state has tried to re-co-opt the symbolism of the Egyptian flag in different ways; the sound of the national anthem played over the radio (see Winegar 2014); and the sonic and visual effects of military aircrafts' emission of plumes of colored smoke intended to draw, in the skies over Cairo, affective symbols for their supporters, such as a white heart and the black, white, and red of the national flag as they flew over pro-Sisi demonstrators in downtown Cairo on July 7, 2013. Military vehicles were also used later during the same summer, exerting not only physical but sonic control over public

Figure 10. Sisi pralines. Photo courtesy of Kalle Laajala.

space. In addition to channeling and symbolizing the hatred a certain portion of the citizenry felt toward pro-Morsi supporters, the military also succeeded in displaying its power to create illusionary stability. In January 25, 2014, military helicopters threw out bundles of flags above Tahrir Square, yet one year later to the day, the same iconic square was shut down, emptied, and silenced, when the state imposed a day of national mourning following the death of King Abdullah of Saudi Arabia. In 2016 and 2017, the state did not even have to impose national mourning on January 25; the square was simply shut down, accompanied by heavy military presence on the ground and in the sky. In 2018, the square was not even shut down by the military. It was just empty, except for a few men dressed in civil clothes—obviously from the security apparatus.

Hence, there are myriad materialized experiences deliberately made under Sisi's leadership that have induced passionate forces of affect among Egyptians, both women and men. We know by now that certain aesthetic politics lead to particular affective responses (see Gregg and Seigworth 2010). As mentioned above, these materialized affective experiences are also linked to how masculinities are made, remade, articulated, and negotiated. However, citizens themselves are also active in the same production. Our senses create affect but also mediate our political and religious consciousness. Resembling findings by the anthropologists Nevena Škrbić Alempijević and Sanja Potkonja in their research on the "Titoaffect," the residual materiality of socialism, and its ambivalent status in Croatia today, in which "for the majority of actors—including researchers—artefacts bearing Tito's image, name or reference to him triggered a strong emotional reaction" (Škrbić Alempijević and Potkonjak 2016, 107), things bearing Sisi's image also triggered people to action.

After the overthrow of Morsi, Bahira Galal (owner of the chocolate shop Kakao in Garden City, Cairo) began printing an edible portrait of Sisi on her chocolate pralines. "I found myself empty-handed at the beginning, until I came up with the idea of using my passion as a tool to share my political leanings to more people—with the help of something everyone loves to eat" (September 24, 2013, *Egypt Independent*). In another article, she stated, "I made these chocolates to express my respect and love for Sisi, who has saved our country" (Galal in El-Behary 2013). When I went to this specific patisserie to buy Sisi pralines (to display when I would later give talks on Egypt) the man behind the desk gave me one for free to taste. This gesture gave me a strong emotional reaction, almost a sense of nausea. Not wanting to be impolite, I did eat the whole praline with Sisi on top. Nevertheless, it was indeed very difficult for me—my body heavily resisted that action of chewing and eating Sisi.

During the fall of 2013, other products followed: Sisi shirts, posters, jewelry, sandwiches (the fast food chain Amo Hosny released the El-Sisi Mix), and even cooking oil. Nermin Nazim, who has created, among other ornaments, pendants bearing the name of Sisi and earrings designed in shape of the Egyptian golden eagle, said, "The army needs our appreciation, and I made this collection of accessories under the name of 'the second victory,' as I believe that the army has achieved the biggest victory since the war of '73.... I'm selling it for very low prices, with only 10 percent profit.... I designed it ... out of my love for our army, not for financial or other reasons" (El-Behary 2013). Journalist Hend El-Behary interviewed Nazim, writing, "She could not hide her love for Sisi, who she says resembles her late father who was an army officer." In the same article, El-Behary interviewed the political and sociological analyst Ammar Ali Hassan, who suggested that the reaction

> relates to people's hunger for a trusted leader that could save them from the ailing country's current situation.... Egyptians have been psychologically suffering because insecurity has been running rampant after the January 25 revolution.... The Egyptian nation is culturally attached to the concept of having a hero, so having a hero like Sisi is particularly important to them.... So far, no other public or political figure with charisma besides Sisi has stepped to the plate.... Sisi used to throw emotional speeches that tickle public sentiments instantly. Moreover Sisi has lavished praise upon Egyptian society to restore lost dignity and nobility, using language that puts himself as the nations' servant. (El-Behary 2013)

The contemporary military-led state of Egypt has harnessed potent forces of affect in ways that continue to mediate political and religious consciousness and masculine bodies, beginning with a number of strategies seen from the summer of 2013 onward.

I assert the significance of the materiality of affect here, that the Sisi pralines are, like the other items, responses to or tangible manifestations of the forces of the summer's affective politics, where love and hate for the country, self, and the other—and an immediate desire for comfort in the face of fear—were urgent (see also Ahmed [2004] and the "inside-out model of emotions," in which affects move from the inside of humans to the outside, toward objects and others). As the literature scholars Dirk Wiemann and Lars Eckstein (2013) note, passion is situated in the relations between porous subjects, and between subjects and objects (read more about the concept of passion in the previous chapters in the book, but especially via the narratives in chapter 1 and chapter 2). The gendered language about heroism is relevant here, discussed below, as is the sensual language of tickling public sentiments and the class-based language of nobility and dignity. These tangible, material manifestations are intimately linked to dominant gender ideologies that re-evolved in mid-August 2013, where the senses may be seen as a window through which to view the changing relationships between subjects and the state.

MORSI'S FAILURES AND SISI'S CONTINUATION OF PREVIOUS POLITICS

To further understand the role of affective politics and the links to masculinities, religion, and nationalism in relation to transformative or static politics in Egypt, we need to take into account Egyptians' increasing sense of political fatigue, and we also must go back in time: from the beginning of 2011, strong forces of affect have been circulating through Egyptians' bodies in an unfamiliar way. In a very short period of time, Egyptians experienced extremes of loss, death, hope, despair, euphoria, and fatigue. Egyptians were, especially after the summer of 2013 and onward, terrified of their own imagined enemies, as mentioned in the previous chapter (see also Hamdy 2012). This terror was an affective response, materialized as an emotion of fear, projected onto neighbors and on persons of different religious and political orientation (see Ahmed 2006), leading to a loss of a sense of security. We must also include Sisi's continuation of the politics introduced by Nasser in forming the modern Egyptian nationhood and, in this regard, in competition with the Muslim Brotherhood and other political Islamic movements, in forming *the* modern national subject, closely linked to models of hegemonic masculinity (see Hirschkind 2004).

President Sisi's politics are more about differing interpretations of the relationship between Islam, nationalism, power, and masculinity than anything else.[3] The current polarization is linked to perceptions of the proper Egyptian Muslim, who in Sisi supporters' vision is one who is patriotic and pro-military, who loves, defends, and believes in Egypt as an autonomous, sovereign country (represented by President Sisi). However, it is not only Muslim Brotherhood supporters but also revolutionaries and liberal activists who are constructed as "enemies" and "terrorists" and suspected of a lack of loyalty to the nation. All categories are perceived as criminals and enemies of the state. Followers of the Muslim Brotherhood, as represented by former President Morsi, are perceived by nationalists as insufficiently patriotic (or not even Egyptian) and as part of a political Islamic movement emotionally oriented toward the global Ummah rather than toward Egypt (see Schielke 2015). For nationalists, the national boundaries must be preserved and secured (this is related not least to the anticolonial movement and history). For many Egyptians, it is imperative that the national boundaries be protected and kept intact—think of the military's involvement in the 1952 revolution, the Sinai Six Days' War in 1967 against Israel, and the resonance of those events with the military's involvement in the 2011 uprising and the battle against political Islam movements, and yet again in the 2013 uprisings and military involvement through to today (in which the Sinai peninsula has also played a crucial role). Moreover, Sisi is following a strategy used by both the Sadat and Mubarak regimes to weaken political opposition; the latter, famously, "had staked its international legitimacy on its claim to be acting as a bulwark against Islamic fundamentalists, particularly the Muslim Brotherhood" (Hirschkind 2012, 50; see Agrama 2012).

Morsi's rule changed over the course of one year; at the beginning it was viewed by my collaborators as similar to Mubarak's political system in terms of its corruption and torture (one often heard the comment that "the only new thing is that they have beards"). But by the end they viewed it as offering worse political leadership than former regimes in terms of security, stability, the economy, infrastructure, and rising sectarian tensions. In October 2012, in a voluble outburst, one taxi driver told me that, in fact, everything had been better under Mubarak. The former regime was corrupt, yes, and there was a growing gap between rich and poor, yes, but people could at least fill their stomachs and had water and electricity. In fact, after June 30, 2013, many taxi drivers I talked to remembered the past *and* Mubarak as a better time with respect to stability and the economic situation. However, some switched their opinions to pro-Morsi arguments after finding out that I was probably not of any danger to them. Setting these emotions in the context of Morsi's 100-day plan, it is not difficult to understand the irony and the core of seriousness in the popular "mango" jokes that cropped up after a TV inter-

view with the president in which he said that during his rule the
mango was affordable and attainable by all. A cynical comparison
between Morsi and Marie Antoinette immediately sprang up on
social media: Let the people eat mango! (instead of bread). Here
again, it is fruitful to think about the materiality of affect—the
ability of mango versus bread in feeding the people of Egypt.
Think also about the 2011 revolts' demands of bread, freedom,
and social justice. It must be said that Morsi retracted several of
his announced changes due to the immediate uproar from the
citizenry, including the proposed substantial tax increase and
price increases for staple foods, and his granting himself unlim-
ited powers by decree at the end of November 2012 (see Malmström 2013a). Morsi was also accused of making purely partisan
appointments of incompetent individuals (see Saad 2013). The
problem of sexual assaults during the protests also continued
during Morsi's rule. As the political scientist and anthropologist
Paul Amar (2013) discusses the active role of the security state in
cultivating a sense of hypermasculinity among the "thugs" and
mobs it mobilized to terrorize protesters. This loud affective
"street masculinity" was linked to the bodies of unemployed
working-class men, particularly youths, in order to harass, sexu-
alize, and torture women and thereby undermine them as political subjects and citizens. Several of my female acquaintances had
been raped or sexually abused during the uprisings (see also
chapter 2). One male friend, Ali, had intervened in a rape on
Mohammed Mahmoud Street in late June 2013 and as a result was
severely beaten. When I met him in July 3, 2013, his face was still
covered with red and blue bruises. What is imperative to note is
that the Tamarod petition actually introduced the security issue
first of all.[4] "Because security has not returned, because the poor
have no place, because I have no dignity in my own country," the

petition reads. "We don't want you anymore." (McTighe 2013). As anthropologist Aymon Kreil noted when he talked about the imagined loss of security in Egypt in May 2013, "Security issues have been directly linked to the perception of unfolding change, and since then the lack of security has remained a common way to criticize its outcomes" (Kreil in Malmström 2013b, 18).

NEO-PATRIARCHY AND AN ICON OF HEGEMONIC MASCULINITY

Sisi's attractiveness and appeal during the time that followed after the summer of 2013 must not be understood as simply a reaction to Morsi's one-year political rule or the extraordinary experiences filled with affective moments of euphoria and horror that the populace lived through. It must also be situated against the background of colonial interference and the many years of postcolonial global interventions in Egypt's national affairs, where collective notions of leadership are linked to perceptions of precise and purposeful manhood. In this sense, emotion traces "a logic in the flesh simultaneously with a logic in history" (Brennan 2004, 116). Of interest here may be the historian Hisham Sharabi's (1992) notion of how the economic, political, social, and cultural changes in the MENA region over the past century have led to the development of "neo-patriarchy." Sharabi affirms that the neo-patriarchal state "is in many ways no more than a modernized version of the traditional patriarchal sultanate" (1992, 7). The anthropologist Suad Joseph (1994) also analyzes the development of state structures in the MENA region, pointing out that state leaders took over kin structures and thereby created a "state patriarchal form."

In contrast with former national leaders, Sisi's political leadership during the first two years was perceived by his followers as both anticolonialist and capable of geopolitically remapping Egypt, shifting the nation away from the West and its former dependence on international institutions like the IMF and the World Bank. In the fall of 2013, Egypt received US$20 billion from its Gulf allies. On August 27, 2013, Egypt rejected an IMF loan after a year of negotiations had proceeded under President Morsi (Bloomberg 2013; see Maxwell 2013). Pro-army Egyptians did not view the cutoff of millions in US aid in October 2013 (Jones 2013; see Beach 2013) in response to the Egyptian military's violent actions toward its people as a problem. On the contrary, it was seen as having opened up room for independence from a former global hegemonic force. At the same time, many of those intellectuals who opposed military dictatorship stressed in January 2015 that everything is a game, a smokescreen that hides continuity in high-level politics. They argued, as do I, that the allies are all the same: Egypt continues to cooperate with the United States, the Gulf invests in Egypt in pursuit of its own regional commercial and political interests, and dependence on the United States remains unchanged. In any case, space opened up during this time for a new strong sense of national self-confidence. For his followers, Sisi became important for a sense of national belonging and dignity (see Al-Ali 2002, Joseph 2000, Kanaaneh et al. 2002).

In Egypt, honor and shame are closely related to dignity and to constructions of gendered person- and nationhood, though not in the way these terms were formerly understood in outdated social science literature (e.g., Gilmore 1987). Honor ideologies have to do with appropriate conduct; they shape interactions between men and women with various identities and selves—that is, they embrace both individual and collective selves. Honor may also be analyzed at the national level, where the group sharing in honor is not the family but the whole nation, which is of particular importance here. An honor code is not a uniform scheme of rules and guidelines but is dynamic and multi-stranded (Baxter 2007; see also Abu-Lughod [2011, 2013] and her critical examinations of honor killings). The gender and sexuality scholar Sherine Hafez's (2012) discussion of multilayered patriarchal power, reversal in the collective consciousness, and uprisings in Egypt is valuable here. She draws on Kandiyoti's term *patriarchal bargain* (a form of negotiation with patriarchal power to describe the relationship between the genders), but the bargain is used here to describe a patriarchal relationship between Egypt's people and its leaders. She points out that in classic Middle Eastern patriarchy "the honor, prestige, and power of the patriarch thus derive from his abilities to provide for as well as to control and ensure the obedience of the members of the group. In this regard, a bargain is struck—not simply one of reciprocal exchange (one of allegiance in return for sustenance) but also one in which inequality is maintained, internalized, and ensured through methods of control" (Hafez 2012, 38). She goes on to observe, "What the events of this uprising [2011] have revealed is that notions of masculinity undermined by a repressive regime have observably shifted the terms of the patriarchal bargain between genders and ages and between the state and its people (Hafez 2012, 39).

For pro-military Egyptians, in mid-August Sisi transformed into a superhero, able to combat both national and international threats. As one female friend, Rania, noted on social media, "Sisi is usually portrayed as a pharaoh and as a figure of the traditional leader[:] caricatures [that carry important] political messages." Sisi's charismatic authority during that time (to use

Max Weber's classic terminology) was partly attached to an imagined decent future, free from unwanted global interventions and free from the Muslim Brotherhood. Among many Egyptians, during his first years of rule Sisi was perceived not only as a strong military male leader, a firm and calming father (following Mubarak, who used the father-and-children metaphor, "legitimized through the construction of mythical power that reined in chaos to ensure the safety and stability of the masses" [Hafez 2012, 39]), but also as the handsome, well-mannered, sexy man and paradigmatic spouse (see Amireh 2003; Hart 2008; Kanafani 2008; Katz 2003; Massad 1995, 2006; on sexuality and masculinities in the MENA region, see, e.g., Bouhdiba [1975] 2012, Kreil 2012, Massad 2007). The anthropologist Farha Ghannam's findings in Egypt also reveal "the parallels people made between a proper government (*hukumah*) and a proper man: protection, support, and provision. This association was clearly reflected in their critique of the previous government and the expectations for the new one as well as how they reimagined the role of the president, the People's Assembly, the police force, and the state more broadly" (2013, 163).

When Sisi came to power, he embodied the proper Muslim man, with a faith that properly embraces love of God and love of the nation. Sisi's followers did not see him as a laughingstock, as Morsi and Mubarak had been perceived (see Malmström 2013a). The desire for national self-confidence is where Morsi failed, not only because of his politics but because he was felt to lack proper masculine leadership traits (see Bier 2011, Rabo 1996). His speeches were viewed as inadequate, repetitive, and stupid, and his weak English skills, body language, and mannerisms were perceived as "low class" among my friends in Egypt.[5]

EGYPT'S AMBIVALENT RELATIONSHIP
WITH THE ARMY

Egypt has been ruled by the military for most of its postindependence existence. The gains of Nasserism diminished significantly in the decades after the imposition of neoliberal reforms with the "opening" of the country to global capital in 1973. But the memory of a military-led state as provider of security and welfare is still strong (if ambivalent), as evidenced by the broad, ongoing support for the military, despite the constantly growing repression by the current government. To understand why proper male subjectivity in Egypt is so thoroughly linked to nationalism and the army, we must first understand the significance of social memory in the national struggle against colonialism and the monarchy. As mentioned above, after the 1952 revolution, the constitutional monarchy was overthrown, along with British colonial influence, and the Nasserist era began.

The politics introduced by this military man were important in forming Egyptian nationhood, especially among the poor (Amin 2000, Hoodfar 1997, Singerman and Hoodfar 1996). For the first time it was possible for lower-income and rural people to achieve upward social mobility through education (Malmström 2016). The "inseparability" of Egyptians from the military is often described; "They are one" was a common refrain in 2013, which echoes a main slogan in Tahrir during the January 25 revolution that was again used by pro-military supporters during the summer of 2013: *El shaab we el geish id wahda*—"The people and the army are one hand." The government plays on these sentiments, using affective politics, through the production or circulation of images and songs. One such instance of the materiality of sonic was the October 2013 "hit" song "Teslam el-`ayaadi" (May these hands be saved), meaning that everything that comes from the military (one of the nation's biggest industrial employers) is blessed.

The military is a repository of national and masculine identity and perhaps the first place where men from poor and rural backgrounds can advance to the highest echelons of the political system (Amin 2000, Hoodfar 1997, Malmström 2016, Singerman and Hoodfar 1996). However, the historian Tewfik Aclimandos (2005) notes that the admitting authorities still examine not only candidates' psychological readiness but also their social origins, which prevents the poor from becoming officers. At the same time, poor young men embody, for the first time in their lives, what is understood to be a fundamental part of the state, and thus they acquire a sense of pride and national belonging—as well as a sense of authority, which is closely connected to ideals of hegemonic masculinity (see Altinay 2004; Enloe 2000; Eriksson Baaz and Stern 2008, 2009, 2010; Higate and Hopton 2005). However, most people have relatives who have been tortured, detained, or killed by the same authorities. Despite this reality, many people resist acknowledging that the military, security, intelligence, and police forces (part of the "deep state" that links together business, military, security, and political elites) form a unified entity and ultimately work together to repress the masses of Egyptians and centralize wealth and power in the hands of the elite.

EMOTIONAL RIFTS

Since the forced dispersal of the sit-ins during the summer of 2013, the state has become more repressive and less responsive to the needs of ordinary Egyptians than at any time in memory. It is deploying unheard-of levels of violence against citizens— from mass murder, in Rabaa' al-Adawiyya and al-Nahda

Squares, to mass incarceration and torture of anyone suspected of challenging the regime. The shooting of female protester Shaima al-Sabbagh, or the Ultras football supporters during early 2015 are examples of the same message: If you are not with us, you are against us. The killing (and brutal torture before his death) of Giulio Regeni, a Cambridge PhD student originally from Italy, when he was conducting fieldwork in Cairo around the January 25 anniversary of "the Arab Spring," took this message to a new level—that non-Egyptians are not safe either. This shift has transformed the affective geography of governance. On anniversaries of sensitive revolutionary dates, when the current regime is extra paranoid, I have noticed an increase in materialized experiences of suspicion (see LeVine and Malmström 2019) devised by the military regime, increasingly explicit every year through 2014, 2015, 2016, and 2018 (I was not in the country in January 2017), such as sophisticated new technologies of surveillance and control (Amar 2013); spatial governmentality, including blocked streets, watchdogs, and checkpoints during night hours (see Ghannam 2013, Ismail 2006); and futuristic (or skull-faced) masks, new uniforms for security personnel, and new armored vehicles, especially in downtown Cairo, but also elsewhere. As one close male friend, Amr, told me in January 2015, referring to the cityscape of downtown Cairo: "They are trying to mute people through the new military machines and masked military. People stay home and [the government] will do whatever they want." The uncertain security situation, interventions by the security police, and the national paranoia have all mutated into a world of suspicion. Highly contagious as they are, these sentiments of suspicion continue to escalate in urgency. People have become hypervigilant. What has developed is a local culture of old-new paranoia (habitual during my fieldwork in 2002–2003) that is being materialized in the cityscape (Malmström et al. 2016).

Immediately after the suppression of the sit-ins and into the fall of 2013, there were fewer nuances between love and hate: it was a period of extremes. While for many during the summer of 2013 the military was a revitalized hope for a better future, by fall 2013 it was beginning to be viewed as somewhat flawed, and increasingly so during 2014 (see Malmström 2014c) and 2015, and "thoroughly" in 2016, 2017, and 2018. By the winter of 2014 and 2015, some people I spoke to had totally changed their minds, while some kept their faith in Sisi (less in 2016, 2017, and 2018). Hence, ambivalences were more explicit in January 2014 (and even more so later on) than they were during the summer of 2013, and the increasingly oppressive and frightening climate (see Gulhane 2014, Hubbard 2013, Jacobs 2013) has created an emotional rift in support for and trust in President Sisi (see Özyürek 2006). As the human rights activist Scott Long (2015), who by then lived in Egypt, expressed it in mid-April 2015: "It [fear] affects every corner of your personality, yet it's hard to take it *personally*, so wide is the danger spread." Life in Egypt during that time was characterized by a plurality of trajectories with conflicting logics that put inhabitants in a state of constant improvisation. During the fall of 2016 and 2017, and during the winter of 2018, the dominant public affect was a complete absence of vitality; instead of intensity, there was anxiety, fear, depression, rage, hopelessness, sense of loss, and fatigue in a context that meant a collapse of the everyday economy and continuous political repression. The government's despotic politics have enhanced national fatigue and political exhaustion and accelerated a movement toward self-imposed exile by many Egyptians. Since the winter of 2015, my friends often expressed this fatigue:

"Now is not the time." "It's not worth it just to be imprisoned or killed." "What point does it make?" Hence, Egyptians live today in a specific setting of uncertainty and escalation of political violence. Let me give one illustrative example with the help of Islam, who is a friend of a friend that I met only once. We had tried to meet several times during one month, but Islam was forced to reschedule every time, since he was extremely busy. He had recently divorced and had two writing jobs to try to support his four children. But he did not manage very well. When I met him, he had just lost his small apartment because he had not been able to pay the rent for the last three months. Islam looked very tired and stressed when we met. He told me about a painful memory from last year when he was arrested. During Ramadan, on a very hot day, he had walked to an ATM machine where he stood in a line for a while. This machine was located close to the parliament building. Suddenly, he lost his temper, and burst out to everyone in the street that the islands belong to Egypt (President Sisi handed the islands Tiran and Sanafir to Saudi Arabia, despite public outcry and court verdicts. See for example Walsh 2017, Al Jazeera 2018). Of course, he was immediately arrested by two policemen and driven to a nearby police station. First, he was blindfolded and interrogated for three hours. The interrogators required that he open his Facebook page. He did, but only the one where he only uploaded posts about football and other nonpolitical updates as well as a photo of himself from national TV. After that, he was treated better and the police chief even removed his handcuffs and let him sit in a chair. Soon thereafter, they placed him alone in a small room, without water and food, until the next afternoon (three o'clock) when they let him go. However, the administration staff gave him both water and food (maybe this was planned and only a game). At the end of our conversation, Islam told me that he clearly had changed, even if it had only been one scary day and night. Islam pointed out that he could not enter that street anymore, and when I asked him why, he said it made him feel too sad. He was also very careful how he acted in public (he self-censored himself) and how he moved in the cityscape of Cairo. He gave me the advice that not to be too paranoid, but to stay constantly vigilant, especially in public rooms.

Even if many Egyptians have lost their faith in Sisi, the majority of those I spoke with continue to perceive the Muslim Brotherhood as enemies. Immediately after the clearing of the sit-ins, many Cairenes were outspoken about their hatred of Morsi and the Muslim Brotherhood. Leyla's voice would change as soon as we talked about that group, and she did not distinguish between them and other Islamic political movements. Surprisingly, Leyla—who views the Muslim Brotherhood as part of a patriarchal system against all Egyptian women—did not talk about Sisi or the military as part of the same system. My friends took it for granted that all poor Egyptians trusted Morsi's politics, casting lower-income Egyptians as easily seduced due to their lack of knowledge and education and their focus on their immediate needs. That said, polarization among Egyptians continues, a process that further develops not only hate and love but also the politics of silence that reemerged during the fall of 2013. I contend that this active silence protects against the open sore of magnified trauma to the collective body. It is also too painful to experience close family members or friends split between Morsi and Sisi supporters. On January 25, 2015, this new silence became explicit in the following scene. I spent the evening and night with experienced male protesters of different generations in an apartment near Tahrir Square, at a time when it was too dangerous to attend any protest in the square because of a ban on protests during the national mourning for King Abdullah of Saudi Arabia. At this gathering no one talked about politics at all. They were mostly silent but gathered together, drinking beer and smoking hashish. They sometimes sang or clapped hands to accompany the tunes of the oud. It was difficult to decide whether this was an act of resistance against the military or whether the men were just drained or coping with the state-forced emptiness and silence of the streets, or both.

POLITICALLY GENDERED BODIES IN FLUX

This concluding chapter has dealt with particular aspects of making and unmaking masculinities in relation to religion, nationalism, and modernity through the lens of the materiality of affect in Egypt. My mode of analysis awakens us to how passion and affective politics ground the political, especially in terms of religion and gender. I have identified certain stimuli and sensations, especially during the summer of 2013, that took on new meanings and produced new forces of affect: the sound of helicopters and the silence during curfew, but also the touch of teargas; the taste of Sisi pralines; the scent and transmission of forces of affect in euphoric, devastated, frightful, and angry political bodies. These experiences fueled a politics of passion after the summer of 2013 that "alert[s] us to the fundamentally public and political status of feeling" (Wiemann and Eckstein 2013, 9). The state's affective politics mold and change Egyptians' bodies in important ways. My argument here is that the nondiscursive experience of affect—the manner in which the forces moving through people produce direct emotional responses—becomes encoded with power and truth claims, thus becoming both discursive and disciplining.

This transformation—the movement whereby the affective becomes the political—continues the circle by amplifying new affective forces. Upon reaching new subjects or objects, these forces are experienced seemingly without mediation, but in fact they carry discursive codes embedded by the myriad forces that shaped them in their travels through various inanimate and human bodies (Malmström, Levine, et al. 2015). This multifaceted and constant interaction helps us also to understand how the production of masculinities is an open-ended life process, actively shaped by both agency and victimhood.

Although it is in many ways a continuation of earlier military governments, the current state has succeeded not only in wielding these strong material and affective forces but also in partly (at least in the beginning) satisfying the widespread desire for stability these forces have evoked. It has done so by reproducing a neo-patriarchal state that is seen as defending national interests, playing on recognizable gender structures and heteronormative expectations and demands of masculinity (which also intersect in important ways with religious imaginaries, bodies, and identities). Thus, the state has both materialized its presence in Cairo and also provoked still more powerful desires for both the individual and collective political body. Or to put it another way, my argument here is that the forces of affective politics, imposed by the potent state, have been circulating and moving in and out of bodies in times of penetrating uncertainty, and they have fed a desire for stable and recognizable structures that are part of the doxic order (yet also have created thick resistance in spaces where avant-garde masculinities continue to be molded). Binary gender structures can be sustained through a reiteration of norms as well as (autonomously) through affect. In times of social and political chaos, seemingly natural identity categories may be imaginative tools for creating stability and stasis. Consequently, the neo-patriarchal state creates and re-creates society's dominant heteronormative expectations and demands. This imagined solidity may also create a potential for individual and collective safety, stability, and comfort, where former neighbors with different religious orientations are transformed into enemies, "non-persons," and terrorists, suspected of a lack of loyalty to the nation (see Bowman 2003). This is an extremely dangerous development that fragments Egyptian civil society, exciting strong emotions of love, hate, and fear as energies that may unite as easily as they fuel further violence. Here, I find Amar's exploration of the logic of hypervisibility and its relation to processes of securitization valuable; drawing on gendered theories of race and coloniality, he shows how "these formations give birth to the parahuman subjects that embody the power of the human-security state" (Amar 2013, 231). The Muslim Brotherhood supporters have become, as I mentioned in the previous chapter, intensely visible as objects of the state, but, as Amar also asserts, "paradoxically, when subjects are hypervisibilized, they remain invisible as social beings: they are not recognizable as complex, legitimate, participatory subjects or citizens" (231–32). Furthermore, we must add the power of global politics. I am drawing on the anthropologist Arjun Appadurai (2006), who asserts that the intensity of today's global processes produces a world of social uncertainty and incompleteness, and when these forms of uncertainties "come into play, violence can create a macabre form of certainty" (Appadurai 2006, 6).

Ironically, today, as Egypt officially rejects a political Islamic masculine identity in relation to governance, it values the same gender ideologies in idealized military leadership; both institutions embrace a masculine ideology where men should be dominant and in control, but also calm, charming, well-mannered, and respectful. In fact, there are more similarities than differences: the Muslim Brotherhood and the army are both hierarchical, authoritarian, and paternalistic institutions. Integral to their ethos is conformity and the dictates of loyalty. Both groups are homophobic and employ antigay politics to "prevent the spread of immorality in society," a continuation of the former regime's politics and ideologies. Thus, the public acceptance of an idealized, masculine, military subjectivity as proper to gendered governance does not differ in some ways from the acknowledgment of idealized, masculine, political-Islamic subjectivity. The present tension and competition between nationalist-military and political-Islamic discourses is actively produced and maintained by military rule, which divides the citizenry into adherents to one of these discourses or the other, enemies to one another, split into rulers and ruled. The brief "artificial" cooperation between the military and (then General) Sisi and the Freedom of Justice Party, the political party of the now-outlawed Muslim Brotherhood movement (under Morsi) now appears unsustainable.

As we know by now, it is not only Muslim Brotherhood supporters who are perceived by the military regime as non persons and noncitizens; revolutionaries and liberal activists are treated in a similar way. Hence, under the current paranoid military dictatorship, these various categories of Egyptian politically opposed citizens have been deemed enemies of the state and have been politically, socially, culturally, and sometimes also physically displaced from spaces and places within their city. Many live in constant fear of arrests, abduction, and detention. But these actors are not silent. As this book has shown, governments can use soundscapes as a form of political control and violence, but my fieldwork in Egypt during the fall and winter of 2016 and onward shows how people also can use sound and sonic resistance to navigate landscapes of insecurity, violence, and displacement, while making room for alternative versions of gender as well. My female and male friends in Cairo claim space through playing cassette-tape sermons in public spaces or through political discussions at home gatherings. Moreover, since 2011, alternative sounds have become an imperative tool for political transformation in Egypt, but also a therapeutic tool. Ethnomusicologist Darci Sprengel, also working in Egypt, wrote to me in the winter of 2018 that she had explored "sound as a sort of artistic therapy to transform public feeling. One of my interlocutors even uses music to go into a state of trance in order to get rid of the panic attacks he started having since 2013 as a result of the political and social violence" (email conversation, December 9, 2018). Hip-hop, punk, and heavy metal are part of the current avant-garde movement, in which some musicians are forced to work in the diaspora whereas others anonymously upload the sonic political messages on YouTube. Politically active women and men listen to these songs at home and even in public (via their earphones) or are themselves part of such music (or theatre, film, poetry) constellations. These sound systems operate at auditory, corporeal, and sociocultural frequencies.

However, even if posttraumatic stress's grip on the collective body has loosened a bit, as mentioned earlier, in the fall of 2017, and during the winter in 2018, the atmosphere was filled with many ambivalent moods, such as depression, stress, and hidden rage. The Cairenes I know acted, moved, and navigated in a novel way; many of the old communities did not exist anymore, and many were not even friends. The irony and the jokes were fewer, and there was simply no money left to "forget the moment for a few hours" and hang out and drink beer every night. Friends, we met earlier in this book, Ahmed, for example, sim-

ply told me: "I am tired of life" and Mohamed, underscored:
"This is the worst time ever in Egypt's history." And as a last
example, my friend, Maged, expressed: "We are living in hell."
The majority told me, without being prompted, that they did
not see any political change for a foreseeable time, maybe at the
earliest in twenty to fifty years. Among my Cairene contacts,
the clear majority who were politically active before and lived
through both joy and despair today talk explicitly about palpable responses (theirs and others') of affective politics such as
suspicion, depression, denial, anger, fatigue, and a sense of
hopelessness that developed after the summer of 2013. They also
note, not only among themselves, how common prescriptions
for psychiatric medication seem to have become since then,
being needed just to cope with everyday life.

To sum up, since 2017, it is possible to grasp the loss of confidence and hope, as well as chronic states of political exhaustion,
fear, suspicion, and mistrust at all levels, including in relation to
the self. During this time, it was also possible to grasp the high
level of collective stress, the daily panic, and the new feeling of
"If you touch me, I will explode." My concluding argument is
that bodies have changed—from collective (in 2011) to individual ones (today). They have been transformed from a collective
confident body of change and an imagined bright better future
to an individual insecure body of control, suspicion, and protection. These men have lost not only hope, but faith as well.
What I experienced during the fall of 2017 and onward, was an
unprotected and "politically mutilated" male body that was in a
constant state of panic because of the collapse of the everyday
economy and political repression. This was a depressed,
stressed out, sprained, and dejected masculine body, stripped of
voice, and trying to control the only thing possible to control:

the flesh, either by building muscles in the gyms or by working harder than ever before to cope with dominant ideologies: to be a breadwinner, to be a proper "real" man. The combination of a collapse of the everyday economy and a total repression of political bodies, especially male bodies, seems to be the perfect recipe to destroy any united opposition or imagination of an alternative better future.[6] When you are economically robbed, you are stripped of your voice, body, and dignity, and you are suspicious of all other political bodies, including your own body. As my friend Mohamed, a former activist, said in the end of November in 2017: "They cut our dicks off in 2013. What is then left?"

We do not yet know how these sensory experiences and the affective politics—including the embracing or opposing of a hegemonic military masculine identity in relation to proper governance—will affect norms that inform masculine trajectories and the diversified category of men on the local level in the future (see Rommel 2015). We must maintain a critical gaze that eschews toxic Orientalist stereotypes and recognize the tension between lived experiences and hegemonic discourses. I agree with the anthropologist Marcia Inhorn (2012) that we must focus on gender in action and explore specific masculine trajectories in relation to time and space (Ghannam 2013).[7] But I would emphasize that we must also explore masculinities in relation to gendered nation-states, religious movements, and so on, also as gendered representatives. As the political scientist Salwa Ismail articulates it: "Gender, as a social category, mediates interaction with the state. In turn, state practices—themselves gendered—shape gender constructions in terms of negotiating masculinity and femininity" (2006, 96). What we do know is that the Egyptian military use of affective politics appears to have deeply molded male bodies, evoking in them powerful responses that continue to play a unique role. As discussed throughout this chapter, these materialized experiences are intimately related to how gendered bodies are produced and reproduced, but also challenged. The dominant public affect of lack of energy and sense of loss (in 2016, 2017, and 2018), in combination with a paranoid military dictatorship's tactics to control its citizens via a collapse of the everyday economy and total repression of political bodies, especially male bodies, produces a public depression and an everyday anxiety that may mold masculine bodies differently.

In the end, the taste of Sisi pralines seems to be more bitter than sweet.

Epilogue

"I am my body," yet in old age my lived body
becomes, paradoxically, "other" than myself.

(Kruks 2010, 273)

SENSORY KNOWLEDGE AND EMOTIVE
ELEMENTS: THE FIELDWORKER

What are the impacts and outcomes of working in affectively demanding and stressful research contexts? What are the sensual resonances? Our research, methodologies, and subsequent writings affect us as researchers and our private life influences our work. That is why I wrote in the preface of this book the somewhat impressionistic and fragmented accounts of my lived fieldwork—from the beginning of this project to its end. For me, it is a requisite, especially so if we are thinking and writing about sensory knowledge and emotive elements and examining the material consequences of the 2011 revolts in Egypt—threatening, uncertain, overwhelming, and even dangerous periods, due not least to the lack of reliable information and to the complex process of interpreting affect—but also the low-intensity post-revolt era under president Sisi, in which things and lived affective experiences induce porous normalcy, suspicion, monotony, boredom, loss, and public depression fleshed out throughout this book. Emotions, which, as we know by now, become tangible through forces of affect, are the sum of many parts, and certainly involve narration, reflection, surmising, and so forth. But key to comprehending how familiar materialities turn ambiguous and how various sentiments seep into the material is, as employed in this book, the transmission of affect (Brennan 2004). This takes place within a wide array of non conscious transactions between people, and between people and their surroundings, but what must not be forgotten is the inclusion of the researcher's body—through which forces of affect flow, molding the individual and collective bodies with which it comes into contact, and the actions in which those bodies engage (Goodman 2012, Massumi 1995).

Conducting fieldwork in violent settings in general is, of course, always demanding, since as ethnographers we are forced to use our own body in the research process, to participate, observe, and distance ourselves at the proper moment. We seldom talk about how such individual experiences enrich us, adding to our professional and private development as well as also wearing us out sometimes—I would say, even remolding us. We become other than ourselves. I do not know yet if using the lens of the new materialism and affect in violent contexts as well as in contexts filled with collective trauma and loss is better or worse than other points of departure. But what I do know is that using my mode of analysis in this project has been both relieving and draining. One lingering affect that I found disturbing—but that has also been beneficial in understanding and in interpreting others' intensely lived experiences during this research—is that although I still have a problem with specific sounds, such as those from helicopters or fireworks, since they make my body feel unsafe, these periods of intense affective politics were easier to endure (see also the discussion about shame and desire in chapter 2) than the calm periods filled with boredom, and hopelessness.

I would like to end this book by again highlighting the value of making explicit the non separation of the scholar's professional body from the private body, since all emotions in relation to other individuals, groups, things, places, and countries affect the analysis and outcome of the research to such a high degree. In my conversations with Professor E. Valentine Daniel of Columbia University during the hot New York City summer of 2016, I tried to convey my ongoing struggles with how to retell or avoid some painful, sometimes unbearable, even politically unmentionable and/or "inappropriate" field data. He suggested (and also wrote a poem based on my fieldwork experiences, which can be read in the beginning of this book) more than once that maybe poetry, verse, photography, and film would be the way to both convey and conserve some of the powerful images and experiences I have witnessed in my project. Doing so may also protect people in political contexts when it is too dangerous to speak, or maybe even when it is too overwhelming for the reader to digest. It may also be the only ethical way to unfold this kind of sensitive field data.

Notes

1. Tamarod (rebellion) was an Egyptian movement critical of President Morsi, created by five activists with support from the left-leaning movements, with the aim of registering opposition to President Morsi and forcing him to call early presidential elections. The movement planned to collect fifteen million signatures by June 30, 2013 (the one-year anniversary of Morsi's inauguration). Tamarod announced that it had collected twenty-two million signatures, not verified, but according to a report by Reuters (Alsharif and Saleh 2013), both police officers and people from the Ministry of the Interior signed, distributed, and collected signatures for the petition (see BBC 2013).

2. All names have been changed in light of the politically sensitive nature of the subject matter. Leyla is my Egyptian friend, and mentor of many years.

3. Already by the end of the fall of 2012 and after one hundred days under the new President Morsi, I wrote about growing "national" hopelessness and about new, growing collective sentiments such as confusion and frustration (Malmström 2013a).

INTRODUCTION

1. History-of-emotions approaches are in dialogue with affect theory, where anthropology's literature on affect and emotion explores how emotion is encoded in language (Besnier 1990), how social discourse determines the way gendered bodies perform and experience affect in everyday life (Lutz and Abu-Lughod 1990), and how public affect (such as fear, anger, grief, hope, and piety) informs modes of sociability (Appadurai 2007, Crapanzano 2003, Herzfeld 2005, Mahmood 2005). Inspired by Spinoza (1677) and Deleuze and Guattari (see, e.g., 1978 and 1987), recent work in social theory extends this research.

2. I am following the body of thoughts of anthropologists such as Appadurai et al. (1986), who made a key turning point within the discipline on the social life of objects, with a number of scholars stressing the inseparability of technology and ontology, of perception and epistemology (Ahmed 2006; Barad 2003; Berlant 2011; Goodman 2009; Ihde 2009; Muñoz 2009; Sterne 2003, 2012; Stewart 2007; Keane 2005; Trovalla and Trovalla 2015). For an excellent overview of artifact-oriented anthropology see Chua and Salmond (2012) and Miller (2005), who argue for various forms of philosophy against the dualism between persons and things in combination with "the messy terrain of ethnography" (Miller 2005, 41).

3. As Frykman emphasizes: "In order to understand the intensity with which affect is evoked by material objects, the relation between the body and the environment needs to be further explored" (Frykman 2016, 154).

4. The members of the World Soundscape Project under the leadership of composer R. Murray Schafer coined the concept in Vancouver in the 1970s.

5. Furthermore, auditory technologies, enable us to hear the imperceptible—such as radioactivity—and the stethoscope aids us in diagnosing illness (see Connor 2004), thus becoming tools for knowing the invisible.

6. Describing listening as method, Kapchan says: "Indeed, learning to listen—as a witness and as a pedagogue—is a *method* that changes the structures and hierarchies of a social field. Listening acts—both

individual and collective—demand an openness to other worlds by obliging the listener to linger in an acoustic space of ambiguity and paradox, a shifting ground wherein preconceived ideas have not yet overdetermined either the subject or the interpretation. Listening to the pain and praise of others can be discomfiting, and yet the decision to intentionally inhabit those sounds is necessarily transformative—not only for the listener and listened-to, but also for the social field of which they are part" (Kapchan 2017, 288).

CHAPTER THREE

An earlier version of this chapter was published in *Anthropology Now* (Malmström 2014b).

1. In the last two decades a rich body of literature has emerged under the rubric of sound studies: the examination of auditory practices and sound environments, and their part in creating senses of self, sociality, and memory (see also Novak and Sakakeeny's (2015) introduction to *Keywords in Sound*, and the entire volume, a noteworthy resource for sound studies, encompassing twenty essays on different sonic topics). Largely inspired by Schafer's (1977) early work, these interdisciplinary studies inquire into the ways that sounds permeate and participate in the creation of place, and the ways they bear upon pressing issues such as ecological, social, and global transformation. Rooted in a broad philosophical interest in the sociopolitical consequences of sound and listening, this emerging body of work shows how the sonic can emplace people in meaningful environments, suffusing them with a sense of home, but also, as shown in this book, how it can participate in campaigns of displacement, creating a sense of vulnerability, fear, and disorientation. Thus, as illustrated by a growing number of scholars in the fields of history (e.g., Smith 2001, Sterne 2003, Thompson 2002) and anthropology (e.g., Feld 1996, Howes 2003), sound, listening, intimacy, affect, and belonging are tightly bound in a co-constitutive relationship (Malmström, Kapchan, et al. 2015). See also Kapchan's (2008, 2009) articles in relation to transnational communities and identity politics.

2. Listening has taken on a great deal of responsibility of late (see Kapchan [2017] for a delicate and stimulating edited volume and an elaboration of the links between sound, theory, method, language, and inscription). In the context of the rise of religiosities, listening is cited as the first step in the processes of conversion (Harding 2000, 59). It makes the subject vulnerable to an interlocutor, opening a space of intersubjectivity and empathetic religious response (Frykholm 2004, 10–11). But listening also has its role in nonreligious world makings. It is foundational in the first awareness of self as sound (Nancy 2007). Through echolocation, listening situates the body within a physical environment and in relation to other sonic agents that populate it. And just as it forms the self, listening can also deform it (Daughtry 2014), sometimes violently (Malmström, Kapchan, et al. 2015).

3. Sound moves through us, and it changes our vibration and rhythm (Connor 2004, Merleau-Ponty 1968). It is tactile. Sound has a touch—the implication of Merleau-Ponty's notions of flesh. Let me explain what I mean: The world is flesh. I am flesh. I share in the exchange of the world. If it is tactile, it is sonic. If it is sonic, it is also affective, in the sense that it performs. Sound affects things as an impulse; it has movement, but it also has an emotional color, a tone (see, e.g., Hackett 2011)—a potential emotional color or tone for or to someone or something in some respect or capacity.

4. Goodman proposes that the two critical tendencies—the politics of silence and the politics of noise—must be supplemented by a politics of frequency, since "the problem of solely prioritizing the amplitude axis (between loudness and quietness) when considering the politics of the sonic intensity is that usually it comes at the expense of a much more complex set of affective resonances distributed across the frequency spectrum" (2012, 65).

CHAPTER FIVE

1. As the anthropologist Arjun Appadurai so well described my book after reading my manuscript the first time.

2. In this chapter I blend theories of affect, new materialism, and dynamic theories of masculinity (Ghannam 2013, Inhorn 2012) into an axis of analysis to help us better understand gender in general, and masculinity in particular. My work is situated within and against the literature on masculinities in general and the construction of military masculinities in particular. Connell's work on hegemonic masculinities is perhaps the best known within the body of literature on masculinities in general. Connell introduces the notion of "hegemonic masculinity," which is defined as "the masculinity that occupies the hegemonic position in a given pattern of gender relations, a position that is always contestable" (1995, 76). Highlighting the hegemonic character of dominant masculinity, however, does not necessarily mean that it is universal, deterministic, or constant through time. Many have argued for attention to multiple masculinities, which are also relational and contextual (Parpart and Zalewski 2008), and this is my point of departure. Recent research on masculinities has indicated that there are often competing notions of masculinities (Ghannam 2013; Inhorn 2012; Ismail 2006; Malmström 2014e, 2015a). Theorizing masculinities—particularly in relation to violence and the military—offers a point of entry into a better understanding of why violent relations seem to be so embedded in notions of romanticized manhood and, therefore, also how they might be constructed differently (see Altinay 2004). For an overview of literature on masculinities and violent conflict, see Stern and Nystrand (2006) and Eriksson Baaz and Stern (2008, 2009). Ghannam's (2013, 2012) ethnographic work in Egypt examines situations in which the use of violence is socially acceptable and even celebrated, as well as situations in which it is socially stigmatized and rejected. She notes that there is a huge difference between being a *gada'*—an honest, brave, reliable, and capable man who uses violence only for its proper purposes—and a *baltagi*—a self-centered thug and bully who uses violence to serve his own interests (Ghannam 2013). In earlier research, I highlighted the role of embodiment in the subjective and intersubjective meaning-making of violence. Experiences of violence are intensely embodied and shape the male body in complex ways. In the specific context of the West Bank, I have argued

that masculinities are often constructed in constant dialogue with violence, pain, and suffering, especially in areas of militarized conflict and politics (Malmström 2014e, 2015a). As Higate and Hopton (2005) suggest, instead of seeing the military as a venue through which boys can achieve their natural potential as men, their research underscores how both genders learn to be "masculine" through methods specifically designed to create soldiers who are able (and willing) to kill to protect the nation. How the military reproduces gendered and sexualized discourses in relation to violence and identities created through them, as well as how gendered discourses reproduce the military and its identities, has been the subject of wide scholarship (see Ackerly, Stern, and True 2006; Stern and Nystrand 2006; Stern and Zalewski 2009). Drawing on Eriksson Baaz and Stern (2008, 2009, 2010; see Enloe 2000; Nordstrom 1998), who point out in their research into constructions of violent militant masculinities the importance of "attention to the intricate interplay between individuals and the discourses that (in part) produce them helps us to see how very fragile even seemingly solid constructions of subjectivity" are (Eriksson Baaz and Stern 2009, 515). Many scholars have discussed the close link between respectable masculinities and nationalism in the Middle East/North African (MENA) region, although I assert here that this link can be understood, in the Egyptian case, only in relation to religion as well (see Altinay 2004; Amireh 2003; Hart 2008; Hirschkind 2004; Kanafani 2008; Massad 1995, 2006; Özyürek 2006; Rommel 2015)—an argument I have made previously about the relationship between Palestinian hegemonic masculinity and nationalism. Work by anthropologist Carl Rommel is imperative if we want to understand "when a new set of subjectivities for how to be an emotional, young and nationalist man were tried out in the realm of Egyptian football" (2015, 282). Furthermore, discursive processes that foreground certain identities and erase others (as we see in today's Egypt) lie at the heart of many national projects (see Bier 2011, Rabo 1996). An especially useful parallel with Egypt's current polarization between the military supporters and Muslim Brotherhood followers is Bowman's (2003) discussion of the imagined violence of a national enemy and nationalisms. Other valuable work on the nation in the MENA area that I draw upon here focuses on the construction of national and collective identity, especially the ways in which gender, the body, emotions, sociability, citizenship, and participation are impacted during moments of transformation (see Al-Ali 2002, Joseph 2000, Kanaaneh 2002). In the MENA region, idealized masculinity, *rujulah*, is closely linked to themes of brave actions, resistance, risk taking, assertiveness, toughness, virility, potency, sacrifice, self-control, paternity, intelligence, valor, generosity, sociality, respect, dignity, and honor. The term is often used to connote men's duty to protect their family honor, *sharaf* (see Gren 2009; Hart 2008; see Kanaaneh 2005; Peteet 1994, 1997). Of course, identity is always a process of becoming and being, and in the Middle East region, as elsewhere, masculinities diverge and are in constant transformation (Abu-Lughod 2011, Amar 2013, Ghannam 2013, Ghoussoub and Sinclair-Webb 2002, Inhorn 2012, Massad 2007, Murray and Roscoe 1997, Ouzgane 2006, Peteet 2007). My analysis follows that of Ghannam, who examines the contradictory, dynamic, and ambiguous process of becoming a man, which she terms the *masculine trajectory*, using an intersectional approach that particularly considers gender and class and the interplay between individual vs. collective, internalized vs. externalized, embodied vs. discursive, and conduct vs. context. Ismail's (2006) analysis of youth activism, gender relations, and state power, and how constructions of masculinity mediate their relations with the state, where the young men embody what she terms an *injured masculinity* that reveals their marginalized position at the same time as they reproduce hegemonic masculinity, provides another theoretical inspiration. Inhorn (2012) similarly pushes for a dynamic theory of masculinity that includes emergent and embodied changes in Middle Eastern manhood and takes new forms of masculine practice seriously. As I have argued elsewhere (Malmström 2014e, 2015a), we must not only affirm the role of embodiment but also understand the production of masculinities as an open-ended life process, actively shaped by both agency and victimhood.

3. See Mahmood's (2012) discussion of secularism, gender, and interreligious sectarian conflict in Egypt.

4. See preface for definition of Tamarod petition.

5. Other leaders within the Muslim Brotherhood were viewed as more competent, e.g., Khairat el-Shater and Mahmoud Ezzat.

6. When I had a discussion with the sociologist Amro Ali in the fall of 2016 about the collapse of the economy in Egypt, he said: "It is not about the economy. It is about ... young people especially hav[ing] lost their connection to the country."

7. The exceptional time (see Scott 2014) of crisis and revolution between 2011 and 2013 was, according to Rommel (2015, 282), "a period when a new set of subjectivities for how to be an emotional, young and nationalist man were tried out in the realm of Egyptian football."

References

Abu-Lughod, Lila. 2011. "Seductions of the 'Honor Crime.'" *Differences* 22 (1): 17–63.

———. 2012. "Living the "Revolution" in an Egyptian Village: Moral Action in a National Space." *American Ethnologist* 39 (1): 21–25.

———. 2013. Do Muslim Women Need Saving. Cambridge, MA: Harvard University Press.

Ackerly, Brooke, Maria Stern, and Jacqui True. 2006. *Feminist Methodologies for International Relations.* Cambridge: Cambridge University Press.

Aclimandos, Tewfik. 2005. "Revisiting the History of the Egyptian Army." In *Re-Envisioning Egypt 1919–1952*, edited by Arthur Goldschmidt and Amy J. Johnson, 68–94. Cairo: American University in Cairo Press.

Agrama, Hussein Ali. 2012. "Reflections on Secularism, Democracy, and Politics in Egypt." *American Ethnologist* 39 (1): 26–31.

Ahmed, Sara. 2004. *The Cultural Politics of Emotion.* New York: Routledge.

———. 2006. *Queer Phenomenology: Orientations, Objects, Others.* Durham, NC: Duke University Press.

Al-Ali, Nadje. 2002. "Between Political Epochs and Personal Lives: Formative Experiences of Egyptian Women Activists." In *Auto/*

biography and the Construction of Identity and Community in the Middle East, edited by Mary Ann Faye, 155–76. New York: Palgrave Macmillan.

Al Jazeera. 2013. "Transcript: Egypt's Army Statement," July 3. Accessed March 25, 2015. http://www.aljazeera.com/news/middleeast/2013/07 /201373203740167797.html.

———. 2018. "Egypt Court Upholds Tiran, Sanafir Transfer to Saudi Arabia," Accessed April 3, 2018. https://www.aljazeera.com/news /2018/03/egypt-court-upholds-tiran-sanafir-transfer-saudi-arabia -180303185036714.html.

Alsharif, Asma, and Yasmine Saleh. 2013. "Special Report: The Real Force behind Egypt's 'Revolution of the State.'" Reuters, October 10. Accessed September 18, 2015. www.reuters.com/article/us-egypt -interior-specialreport-idUSBRE99908D20131010.

Altinay, Ayse Gul. 2004. *The Myth of the Military-Nation: Militarism, Gender, and Education in Turkey*. New York: Palgrave Macmillan.

Amar, Paul. 2013. *The Security Archipelago: Human-Security States, Sexuality Politics, and the End of Neoliberalism*. Durham, NC: Duke University Press.

Amin, Galal. 2000. *Whatever Happened to the Egyptians? Changes in Egyptian Society from 1950 to the Present*. Cairo: The American University in Cairo Press.

Amireh, Amal. 2003. "Between Complicity and Subversion: Body Politics in Palestinian National Narrative." *South Atlantic Quarterly* 102 (4): 747–72.

Appadurai, Arjun. 1986. "Introduction: Commodities and the Politics of Value." In *The Social Life of Things*, edited by Arjun Appadurai, 3–63. Cambridge: Cambridge University Press.

———. 2006. *Fear of Small Numbers: An Essay on the Geography of Anger*. Durham, NC: Duke University Press.

———. 2007. "Hope and Democracy," *Public Culture* 19 (1): 29–34.

Armstrong, Robert Plant. 1981. *Powers of Presence: Consciousness, Myth and Affecting Presence*. Philadelphia: University of Pennsylvania Press.

Auslander, Leora. 2005. "Beyond Words." *American Historical Review* 110 (4):1015–45.

Barad, Karen. 2003. "Posthumanist Performativity: Toward and Understanding of How Matter Comes to Matter." *Signs: Journal of Women in Culture and Society* 28 (3): 801–31.

Bartels, Anke, 2013. "'The East Is Red': The Politics of Mobilising Passion in the Chinese Cultural Revolution." In *The Politics of Passion: Reframing Affect and Emotion in Global Modernity*, edited by Dirk Wiemann and Lars Eckstein, 35–50. Frankfurt: Peter Lang Academic Research.

Barthes, Roland. 1981. *Camera Lucida: Reflections of Photography.* New York: Hill and Wang.

Baxter, Diane. 2007. "Honor thy Sister: Selfhood, Gender, and Agency in Palestinian Culture." *Anthropological Quarterly* 80 (3): 737–75.

BBC. 2012. "Egyptian 'Battle of the Camels' officials acquitted," October 10. Accessed May 5, 2017. http://www.bbc.com/news/world-middle-east-19905435.

———. 2013. "Egypt's Tamarod Protest Movement," July 1. Accessed March 25, 2015. http://www.bbc.com/news/world-middle-east-23131953.

Beach, Alistair. 2013. "General Abdel Fattah al-Sisi: The Many Faces of Egypt's Presidential Possibility." *The Independent*, October 16. Accessed October 16, 2013. http://www.independent.co.uk/news/world/africa/general-abdel-fattah-alsisi-the-many-faces-of-egypts-presidential-possibility-8883788.html.

Bennett, Jane. 2010. *Vibrant Matter: A Political Ecology of Things.* Durham, NC: Duke University Press.

Bergson, Henri. 1896. *Matter and Memory.* Translated by Nancy Margaret Paul and Scott Palmer. Reprint, New York: Zone Books, 1996.

———. 2007. *Matter and Memory.* New York: Cosimo Books.

Berlant, Laureen. 2011. *Cruel Optimism.* Durham, NC: Duke University Press.

Besnier, N. 1990. "Language and Affect." *Annual Review of Anthropology* 19: 419–51.

Biddle, Ian, and Marie Thompson. 2013. *Sound, Music, Affect: Theorizing Sonic Experience*, edited by Ian Biddle and Marie Thompson. New York: Bloomsbury.

Bier, Laura. 2011. *Revolutionary Womanhood: Feminisms, Modernity, and the State in Nasser's Egypt.* Stanford, CA: Stanford University Press.

Bille, Mikkel, Frida Hastrup, and Tim Flohr. 2010. *An Anthropology of Absence: Materializations of Transcendence and Loss.* London: Springer.

Blackman, Lisa, and Couze Venn. 2010. "Affect." *Body & Society* 16 (1): 7–28.

Bloomberg News. 2013. "Egypt Turns Back on IMF and Looks to Gulf for Stimulus." *The National,* August 30. Accessed August 30, 2013. http://www.thenational.ae/featured-content/channel-page/business/middle-article-list/egypt-turns-back-on-imf-and-looks-to-gulf-for-stimulus.

Bouhdiba, Abdelwahab. (1975) 2012. *Sexuality in Islam.* Translated by Alan Sheridan. London: Saqi Books.

Bourdieu, Pierre. 1977. *Outline of a Theory of Practice.* Translated by Richard Nice. Cambridge: Cambridge University Press.

Bowman, Glenn. 2003. "Constitutive Violence and the Nationalist Imaginary: Antagonism and Defensive Solidarity in 'Palestine' and 'Former Yugoslavia.'" *Social Anthropology* 11 (3): 319–40.

Braidotti, Rosi. 2010. "The Politics of 'Life Itself' and New Ways of Dying." In *New Materialisms: Ontology, Agency, and Politics,* edited by Diana Coole and Samantha Frost, 201–18. Durham, NC: Duke University Press.

———. 2013. *The Posthuman.* Cambridge: Polity.

Brennan, Teresa. 2004. *Transmission of Affect.* Ithaca, NY: Cornell University Press.

Brodwin, Paul E. 1994. "Symptoms and Social Performances: The Case of Diane Reden." In *Pain as a Human Experience: An Anthropological Perspective,* edited by Mary-Jo DelVecchio, Paul E. Brodwin, Byron J. Good, and Arthur Kleinman, 77–100. Berkeley: University of California Press.

Casey, Edward S. 1987. *Remembering: A Phenomenological Study.* Bloomington: Indiana University Press.

Chua, Liana, and Amira Salmond. 2012. "Artefacts in Anthropology." In *The Sage Handbook of Social Anthropology,* vol. 2, edited by Richard Fardon, Oliva Harris, Trevor H.J. Marchand, Cris Shore, Veronica

Strang, Richard Wilson, and Mark Nuttall, 1–17. Thousand Oaks, CA: Sage.

Cole, Teju. 2015. "Object Lesson." *New York Times Magazine*, March 22, 2015. Accessed November 20, 2015. http://www.nytimes.com/2015/03/22/magazine/object-lesson.html?rref=collection%2Fcolumn%2Fon-photography&action=click&contentCollection=magazine&region=stream&module=stream_unit&version=latest&contentPlacement=8&pgtype=collection.

Connell, R. W. 1995. *Masculinities*. Los Angeles: Polity Press.

Connor, Steven. 2004. "Edison's Teeth: Touching Hearing." In *Hearing Cultures: Essays on Sound, Listening, and Modernity*, edited by Veit Erlmann, 153–72. Oxford: Berg Publishers.

Coole, Diana. 2010. "The Inertia of Matter and the Generativity of Flesh." In *New Materialisms: Ontology, Agency, and Politics*, edited by Diana Coole and Samantha Frost, 92–115. Durham, NC: Duke University Press.

Coole, Diana, and Samantha Frost. 2010. "Introducing the New Materialisms." In *New Materialisms: Ontology, Agency, and Politics*, edited by Diana Coole and Samantha Frost, 1–46. Durham, NC: Duke University Press.

Crapanzano, V. 2003. "Reflections on Hope as a Category of Social and Psychological Analysis." *Cultural Anthropology* 18 (1): 3–32.

Crossland, Zoe. 2002. "Violent Spaces: Conflict over the Reappearance of Argentina's Disappeared." In *Matériel Culture: The Archaeology of Twentieth-Century Conflict*, edited by John Schofield, William Gray Johnson, and Colleen M. Beck, 115–31. London: Routledge.

Das, Veena. 1995. *Critical Events: An Anthropological Perspective on Contemporary India*. Delhi: Oxford University Press.

Daughtry, J. Martin. 2014. "Thanatosonics: Ontologies of Acoustic Violence." *Social Text* 32 (2): 25–51.

De Botton, Alain. 1997. *How Proust Can Change Your Life*. New York: Vintage International.

Deleuze, Gilles. 1978. "Lecture Transcripts on Spinoza's Concept of Affect." *Les Cours de Gilles Deleuze*. Accessed June 20, 2015. http://www.gold.ac.uk/media/images-by-section/departments/research

-centres-and-units/research-centres/centre-for-invention-and
-social-process/deleuze_spinoza_affect.pdf.

———. 1986. *Cinema 1: The Movement-Image.* Translated by Hugh Tomlinson and Barbara Habberjam. Minneapolis: University of Minnesota Press.

———. 1989. *Cinema 2: The Time-Image.* Translated by Hugh Tomlinson and Robert Galeta. Minneapolis: University of Minnesota Press.

Deleuze, Gilles, and Félix Guattari. 1987. *A Thousand Plateaus: Capitalism and Schizophrenia.* Minneapolis: University of Minnesota Press.

Douglas, Mary. 1966. *Purity and Danger: An Analysis of the Concepts of Pollution and Taboo.* London: Routledge.

Duff, Cameron. 2010. "On the Role of Affect and Practice in the Production of Place." *Environment and Planning D: Society and Space* 28: 881–95.

Edwards, Christina. 2014. "Material Memories: The Making of a Collodion Memory-Text." In *Love Objects: Emotion, Design and Material Culture,* edited by Anna Moran and Sorcha O'Brien, 113–23. London: Bloomsbury.

El-Behary, Hend. 2013. "'Sisi Fever' Makes Its Mark on Random Egyptian Products." *Egypt Independent,* August 11. Accessed November 20, 2015. http://www.egyptindependent.com/news/%E2%80%98sisi
-fever-makes-its-mark-random-egyptian-products.

Empson, Rebecca. 2007. "Differentiation and Encompassment: A Critique of Alfred Gell's Theory of the Abduction of Creativity." In *Thinking through Things: Theorising Artefacts Ethnographically,* edited by Amiria Henare, Martin Holbraad, and Sari Wastell, 113–40. London: Routledge.

Enloe, Cynthia. 2000. *Maneuvers: The International Politics of Militarizing Women's Lives.* Berkeley: University of California Press.

Eriksson Baaz, Maria, and Maria Stern. 2008. "Making Sense of Violence: Voices of Soldiers in the DRC." *Journal of Modern African Studies* 46 (1): 57–86.

———. 2009. "Why Do Soldiers Rape? Gender, Violence and Sexuality in the DRC Armed Forces." *International Studies Quarterly* 53 (3): 495–518.

————. 2010. "The Complexity of Violence: A Critical Analysis of Sexual Violence in the Democratic Republic of Congo (DRC)." Working Paper on Gender Based Violence. The Nordic Africa Institute and Sida. Stockholm, May 2010.

Fahmy, Ziad. 2013. "Coming to Our Senses: Historicizing Sound and Noise in the Middle East." *History Compass* 11 (4): 305–15.

Feld, Steven. 1996. "Waterfalls of Song: An Acoustemology of Place Resounding in Bosavi, Papua New Guinea." In *Senses of Place*, edited by Steven Feld and Keith Basso, 91–135. Santa Fe, NM: School of American Research Press.

Fowles, Severin. 2010. "People without Things." In *An Anthropology of Absence: Materializations of Transcendence and Loss*, edited by Mikkel Bille, Frida Hastrup, and Tim Flohr, 23–41. London: Springer.

Frost, Samantha. 2010. "Fear and the Illusion of Autonomy." In *New Materialisms: Ontology, Agency, and Politics*, edited by Diana Coole and Samantha Frost, 92–115. Durham, NC: Duke University Press.

Frykholm, Amy Johnson. 2004. *Rapture Culture: Left Behind in Evangelical America*. New York: Oxford University Press.

Frykman, Jonas. 2016. "Done by Inheritance. A Phenomenological Approach to Affect and Material Culture." In *Sensitive Objects: Affect and Material Culture*, edited by Jonas Frykman and Maja Povrzanović Frykman, 153–179. Lund: Nordic Academic Press.

Frykman, Jonas, and Maja Povrzanović Frykman. 2016. "Affect and Material Culture. Perspectives and Strategies." In *Sensitive Objects: Affect and Material Culture*, edited by Jonas Frykman and Maja Povrzanović Frykman, 9–31. Lund: Nordic Academic Press.

Gell, Alfred. 1998. *Art and Agency: An Anthropological Theory*. Oxford: Oxford University Press.

Ghannam, Farha. 2012. "Meanings and Feelings: Local Interpretations of the Use of Violence in the Egyptian Revolution." *American Ethnologist* 39 (1): 32–36.

————. 2013. *Live and Die Like a Man: Gender Dynamics in Urban Egypt*. Stanford, CA: Stanford University Press.

Ghoussoub, Mai, and Emma Sinclair-Webb. 2002. *Imagined Masculinities: Male Identity and Culture in the Modern Middle East.* London: Saqi Books.

Gilje, Nils. 2016. "Moods and Emotions. Some Philosophical Reflections on the 'Affective Turn.'" In *Sensitive Objects: Affect and Material Culture,* edited by Jonas Frykman and Maja Povrzanović Frykman, 31–55. Lund: Nordic Academic Press.

Gilmore, David D. 1987. *Honor and Shame and the Unity of the Mediterranean,* Washington, DC: American Anthropological Association.

Goodman, Steve. 2009. "Contagious Noise." In *Spam Book: On Viruses, Porn, and Other Anomalies from the Dark Side of Digital Culture,* edited by Tony Sampson and Jussi Parikka, 125–40. Cresshill, NJ: Hampton Press.

———. 2012. *Sonic Warfare: Sound, Affect and the Ecology of Fear.* Cambridge, MA: MIT Press.

Gordillo, Gastón R. 2014. *Rubble: The Afterlife of Destruction.* Durham, NC: Duke University Press.

Gregg, Melissa, and Gregory J. Seigworth. 2010. "An Inventory of Shimmers." In *The Affect Theory Reader,* edited by Melissa Gregg and Gregory J. Seigworth, 1–28. Durham, NC: Duke University Press.

Gren, Nina. 2009. "Each Day Another Disaster: Politics and Everyday Life in a Palestinian Refugee Camp in the West Bank." PhD diss., School of Global Studies, University of Gothenburg.

Grosz, Elizabeth. 2010. "Feminism, Materialism and Freedom." In *The New Materialisms: Ontology, Agency, and Politics,* edited by Diana Coole and Samantha Frost, 139–57. Durham, NC: Duke University Press.

Gulhane, Joel. 2014. "Egypt President Sends Letter to Family of Imprisoned Al Jazeera Journalist" *Daily News,* March 18. Accessed March 18, 2014. http://www.dailynewsegypt.com/2014/03/18/egypt-president-sends-letter-family-imprisoned-al-jazeera-journalist.

Hackett, Rosalind I.J. 2011. "Auditory Materials." In *The Routledge Handbook of Research Methods in the Study of Religion,* edited by Michael Stausberg and Steven Engler, 447–58. London: Routledge.

Hafez, Sherine. 2012. "No Longer a Bargain: Women, Masculinity, and the Egyptian Uprising." *American Ethnologist* 39 (1): 37–42.

Hamdy, Sherine, F. 2012. "Strength and Vulnerability after Egypt's Arab Spring Uprisings." *American Ethnologist* 39 (1): 43–48.

Harding, Susan. 2000. *The Book of Jerry Falwell: Fundamentalist Language and Politics*. Princeton, NJ: Princeton University Press.

Hart, Jason. 2008. "Dislocated Masculinity: Adolescence and the Palestinian Nation-in-Exile." *Journal of Refugee Studies* 21 (1): 64–81.

Hauge, Elisabeth Sørfjorddal. 2016. "In the Mood: Place and Tools in the Music Industry with a Focus on Entrepreneurship." In *Sensitive Objects: Affect and Material Culture*, edited by Jonas Frykman and Maja Povrzanović Frykman, 199–215. Lund: Nordic Academic Press.

Hauslohner, Abigail, and Sharaf al-Hourani. 2013. "Fall-Off in Egyptian Protests as Army Stays Silent on Total Killed or Arrested." *The Guardian*, September 3. Accessed October 15, 2013. http://www.theguardian.com/world/2013/sep/03/egyptian-protests-muslim-brotherhood-military.

Heidegger, Martin. 1996. *Being and Time*. Albany: State University of New York Press.

Henare, Amiria, Martin Holbraad, and Sari Wastell. 2007. "Introduction: Thinking through Things." In *Thinking through Things: Theorising Artefacts Ethnographically*, edited by Amiria Henare, Martin Holbraad, and Sari Wastell, 1–31. London: Routledge.

Henriques, Julian. 2011. *Sonic Bodies: Reggae Sound Systems, Performance Techniques and Ways of Knowing*. New York: Continuum Press.

Herzfeld, M. 2005. *Cultural Intimacy: Social Poetics in the Nation-State*. New York: Routledge.

Higate, Paul, and John Hopton. 2005. "War Militarism and Masculinities." In *Handbook of Studies on Men and Masculinities*, edited by Michael Kimmel, Jeff Hearn, and R. W. Connell, 432–48. London: Sage.

Hirschkind, Charles. 2004. "Hearing Modernity: Egypt, Islam, and the Pious Ear." In *Hearing Cultures: Sound, Listening, and Modernity*, edited by V. Erlmann, 131–51. New York: Berg Publishers.

———. 2006. *The Ethical Soundscape: Cassette Sermons and Islamic Counterpublics*. New York: Columbia University Press.

———. 2012. "Beyond Secular and Religious: An Intellectual Genealogy of Tahrir Square." *American Ethnologist* 39 (1): 49–53.

Hoodfar, Homa. 1997. *Between Marriage and the Market: Intimate Politics and Survival in Cairo*. Berkeley: University of California Press.

Howes, David. 2003. *Sensual Relations: Engaging the Senses in Culture and Social Theory*. Ann Arbor: University of Michigan Press.

Hsu, Elisabeth. 2000. "Towards a Science of Touch. Part 1: Chinese Pulse Diagnostics in Early Modern Europe." *Anthropology & Medicine* 7 (2): 251–68.

———. 2008. "The Senses and the Social: An Introduction." *Ethnos* 73 (4): 433–43.

Hubbard, Ben. 2013. "American Held in Egypt Killed Himself, Officials Say." *New York Times*, October 20. Accessed October 20, 2013. http://www.nytimes.com/2013/10/14/world/middleeast/egyptian-officials-say-american-killed-himself-in-prison.html?_r=0.

Human Rights Watch. 2014a. "Egypt: Rab'a Killings Likely Crimes against Humanity," August 12. Accessed March 25, 2015. http://www.hrw.org/news/2014/08/12/egypt-rab-killings-likely-crimes-against-humanity.

———. 2014b. "All According to Plan. The Rab'a Massacre and Mass Killings of Protesters in Egypt," Accessed June 8, 2015. http://www.hrw.org/reports/2014/08/12/all-according-plan-0.

Ihde, Don. 2009. *Postphenomenology and Technoscience: The Peking University Lectures*. New York: State University of New York Press.

Inhorn, Marcia, C. 2012. *The New Arab Man: Emergent Masculinities, Technologies, and Islam in the Middle East*. Princeton, NJ: Princeton University Press.

Ismail, Salwa. 2006. *Political Life in Cairo's New Quarters: Encountering the Everyday State*. Minneapolis: University of Minnesota Press.

Jacobs, Harrison. 2013. "Two Canadians Describe the Harrowing 51 Days They Spent in an Egyptian Prison." *Business Insider*, October 17. Accessed June 4, 2017. http://www.businessinsider.com/canadians-describe-egyptian-prison-2013-10.

Jansen, Stef. 2016. "Ethnography and the Choices Posed by the 'Affective Turn.'" In *Sensitive Objects: Affect and Material Culture*, edited by Jonas Frykman and Maja Povrzanović Frykman, 55–79. Lund: Nordic Academic Press.

Johansen, R. Elise. 2002. "Pain as a Counterpoint to Culture: Towards and Analysis of the Experience of Pain in Infibulation among African Immigrants in Norway." *Medical Anthropology Quarterly* 16 (3): 312–40.

Jones, Sophia. 2013. "General Al-Sisi's Popularity Soars after U.S. Aid Cut-Off to Egypt." *Daily Beast*, October 10. Accessed October 10, 2013. http://www.thedailybeast.com/articles/2013/10/10/general-al-sisi-s-popularity-soars-after-u-s-aid-cut-off-to-egypt.html.

Joseph, Suad. 1994. "Brother/Sister Relationships: Connectivity, Love, and Power in the Reproduction of Patriarchy in Lebanon." *American Ethnologist* 21 (1): 50–73.

————, ed. 2000. *Gender and Citizenship in the Middle East.* Syracuse, NY: Syracuse University Press.

Kanaaneh, Rhoda. 2002. *Birthing the Nation: Strategies of Palestinian Women in Israel.* Berkeley: University of California Press.

————. 2005. "Boys or Men? Duped or 'Made'? Palestinian Soldiers in the Israeli Military." *American Ethnologist* 32 (2): 2607–5.

Kanafani, Samar. 2008. "Leaving Mother-Land: The Anti-Feminine in Fida'i Narratives." *Identities* 15 (3): 297–316.

Kapchan, Deborah. 2008. "The Promise of Sonic Translation: Performing the Festive Sacred in Morocco." *American Anthropologist* 110: 467–83.

————. 2009. "Singing Community/Remembering in Common: Sufi Liturgy and North African Identity in Southern France." *International Journal of Community Music* 2 (1): 9–23.

————. 2014. "Welcoming Remarks and Introduction Day 1." In *The Materiality of Affect in North Africa: Politics in Flux*, edited by Maria Frederika Malmström and Deborah Kapchan. Workshop and Roundtable Report, October 3–4, 2014, New York University, New York. Accessed June 20, 2015. http://nai.diva-portal.org/smash/get/diva2:814003/FULLTEXT01.pdf.

————. 2015. "Body." In *Keywords in Sound*, edited by David Novak and Matt Sakakeeny, 33–44. Durham, NC: Duke University Press.

————. 2017. "Listening Acts: Witnessing the Pain (and Praise) of Others." In *Theorizing Sound Writing*, edited by Deborah Kapchan, 277–94. Middletown, CT: Wesleyan University Press.

Kapferer, Bruce. 2015. "Introduction: In the Event—toward an Anthropology of Generic Moments." In *In the Event: Toward an Anthropology of Generic Moments*, edited by Bruce Kapferer and Lotte Meinert, 1–27. New York: Berghahn Books.

Katz, Sheila H. 2003. *Women and Gender in Early Jewish and Palestinian Nationalism*. Gainesville: University Press of Florida.

Keane, Webb. 2005. "Signs Are Not the Garb of Meaning: On the Social Analysis of Material Things." In *Materiality*, edited by Daniel Miller, 182–205. Durham, NC: Duke University Press.

Kingsley, Patrick. 2013. "Eye Sniper of Tahrir Square is in Jail, but has Anything Changed?" *The Guardian*, March 6. Accessed September 1, 2016. https://www.theguardian.com/world/shortcuts/2013/mar/06/eye-sniper-tahrir-egypt-jailed.

Kreil, Aymon. 2012. "Du rapport au dire: Sexe, amour et discours d'expertise au Caire." PhD diss., Paris: EHESS, Neuchâtel.

———. 2014. "Love Scales: Class and Expression of Feelings in Cairo." *La Ricerca Folklorica* 69: 83–91.

———. 2016a. "Territories of Desire: A Geography of Competing Intimacies in Cairo." *Journal of Middle East Women's Studies* 12 (2): 166–80.

———. 2016b. "The Price of Love: Valentine's Day and Its Enemies in Egypt," *Arab Studies Journal* 24 (2): 128–46.

Kristeva, Julia. 1982. *Powers of Horror: An Essay on Abjection*. Translated by Leon S. Roudiez. New York: Columbia University Press.

Kruks, Sonia. 2010. "Simone de Beauvoir: Engaging Discrepant Materialisms." In *New Materialisms: Ontology, Agency, and Politics*, edited by Diana Coole and Samantha Frost, 258–80. Durham, NC: Duke University Press.

Kusenbach, Margarethe. 2003. "Street Phenomenology: The Go-Along as Ethnographic Research Tool" *Ethnography* 4 (3): 455–85.

LaBelle, Brandon. 2006. *Background Noise: Perspectives on Sound Art*. New York: Continuum Books.

———. 2010. *Acoustic Territories: Sound Culture and Everyday Life*. New York: Continuum.

———. 2012. *Diary of an Imaginary Egyptian*. Berlin: Errant Bodies Press.

Latour, Bruno. 2004. *Politics of Nature: How to Bring the Sciences into Democracy.* Translated by Catherine Porter. Cambridge, MA: Harvard University Press.

Leach, James. 2007. "Differentiation and Encompassment: A Critique of Alfred Gell's Theory of the Abduction of Creativity." In *Thinking through Things: Theorising Artefacts Ethnographically*, edited by Amiria Henare, Martin Holbraad, and Sari Wastell, 167–88. London: Routledge.

LeVine, Mark. 2008. *Heavy Metal Islam: Rock, Resistance, and the Struggle for the Soul of Islam.* New York: Three Rivers Press.

—. Producer. 2013. Film: *Before the Spring, After the Fall.* Directed by Jed Rothstein. USA: Anthro Films/HMI Productions/Insurgent Media.

LeVine, Mark, and Maria Frederika Malmström. 2019. "Understanding the Materiality of Suspicion: Affective Politics in MENA Cities." In *Routledge Handbook on Middle East Cities*, edited by Haim Yacobi and Mansour Nasasra. London. Routledge.

Linos, Natalia. 2010. "Reclaiming the Social Body through Self-Directed Violence." *Anthropology Today* 26 (5): 8–12.

Long, Scott. 2015. "Deport Me!" *A Paper Bird Blog.* April 18, 2015. Accessed April 20, 2015. https://paper-bird.net/2015/04/.

Lutz, Catherine A., and Lila Abu-Lughod. 1990. "Language and the Politics of Emotion." In *Studies in Emotion and Social Interaction*, edited by Lila Abu-Lughod and Catherine A. Lutz, 979–80. Cambridge: Cambridge University Press.

Mahmood, Saba. 2005. *Politics of Piety. The Islamic Revival and the Feminist Subject.* Princeton, NJ: Princeton University Press.

—. 2012. "Sectarian Conflict and Family Law in Contemporary Egypt." *American Ethnologist* 39 (1): 54–62.

Malmström, Maria Frederika. 2013a. "Ihbaat Again? Ihbaat—Frustration—Is One of the Emotions in Play as Egyptian People Try to Cope with Their New Political Circumstances." In *Development Dilemmas: Annual Report 2012*, 37–42. Uppsala: The Nordic Africa Institute. Accessed June 4, 2017. http://www.nai.uu.se/about/organisation/annualreport/NAI_2012AnnualReport_HighRes.pdf.

———. 2013b. "Introduction." In Affective Politics in Transitional North Africa: Imagining the Future, edited by Maria Frederika Malmström. Workshop and Roundtable Report, Conflict, Displacement and Transformation conference proceedings, May 27–28, 2013, Alexandria, Egypt. Uppsala: The Nordic Africa Institute. Accessed June 20, 2015. http://nai.diva-portal.org/smash/get/diva2:693357/FULLTEXT01.pdf.

———. 2014a. "Feature Preview. The Sound of Silence." *Anthropology Now*, January 7. Accessed June 20, 2015. http://anthronow.com/print/feature-preview-sound-of-silence.

———. 2014b. "The Sound of Silence in Cairo: Affect, Politics and Belonging." *Anthropology Now* 6 (2): 23–34.

———. 2014c. "Egypt in Motion." Visual and New Media Review, *Cultural Anthropology*, May 26. Accessed March 19, 2015. http://www.culanth.org/fieldsights/534-egypt-in-motion.

———. 2014d. "Introduction." In *Politics in Transitional North Africa: Imagining the Future*, edited by Maria Frederika Malmström. Workshop and Roundtable Report, 27–28 May 2013, 7–8. Alexandria, Egypt: The Nordic Africa Institute. Accessed March 26, 2014. http://nai.diva-portal.org/smash/get/diva2:693357/FULLTEXT01.pdf.

———. 2014e. "Making Uncertain Manhood: Masculinities, Embodiment and Agency among Male Hamas Youth." In *Embodiments, Discourses and Symbolic Practices*, edited by Georg Frerks, Reinhilde König, and Annelou Ypeij. Ashgate Series of Gender in a Global/Local World. London: Ashgate Press.

———. 2015a. "Porous Masculinities: Agential Political Bodies among Male Hamas Youth." *Etnográfica* 19 (2): 301–22.

———. 2016. *The Politics of Female Circumcision in Egypt: Gender, Sexuality and the Construction of Identity*. London: I. B. Tauris.

———. Forthcoming. "The Body of Change: An Ethnography of the Material Affects of Military Intervention." In *Material Aspects of Public Affect: Social Transformations in Qualitative Research*, edited by Aymon Kreil, Yasmine Berriane, Annuska Derks and Dorothea Lüddeckens. New York: Palgrave Macmillan.

Malmström, Maria Frederika, Deborah Kapchan, J. Martin Daughtry, and Owe Ronström. 2015. Proposal, "Listening to Home: A Comparative Soundscape Study." Riksbankens Jubileumsfond.

Malmström, Maria Frederika, Mark LeVine, Ulrika Trovalla, and Eric Trovalla. 2015. Proposal: "The Materiality of Suspicion and the Ambiguity of the Familiar in Nigeria and Egypt." Riksbankens Jubileumsfond.

————. 2016. Proposal: "The Materiality of Suspicion and the Ambiguity of the Familiar: Nigerian and Egyptian Cityscapes." Vetenskapsrådet.

Massad, Joseph A. 1995. "Conceiving the Masculine: Gender and Palestinian Nationalism." *Middle East Journal* 49 (3): 467–83.

————. 2006. *The Persistence of the Palestinian Question: Essays on Zionism and the Palestinians.* London: Routledge.

————. 2007. *Desiring Arabs.* Chicago: Chicago University Press.

Massumi, Brian. 1995. "The Autonomy of Affect." *Cultural Critique* (The Politics of Systems and Environments, Part II) 31: 83–109.

————. 2002. *Parables for the Virtual: Movement, Affect, Sensation.* Durham, NC: Duke University Press.

Maxwell, James. 2013. "Can Gulf Money Save Egypt's Economy?" *Think Africa Press,* October 2. Accessed October 2, 2013. http://thinkafricapress.com/egypt/can-gulf-money-save-economy.

McTighe, Kristen. 2013. "Egypt's 'Rebels' Aim to Oust Morsi with Petition, Protests." *GlobalPost,* June 27. Accessed May 15, 2017. https://www.pri.org/stories/2013-06-27/egypts-rebels-aim-oust-morsi-petition-protests.

Merleau-Ponty, Maurice. 1968. *The Visible and the Invisible.* Translated by Alphonso Lingis. Evanston, IL: Northwestern University Press.

Miller, Daniel. 2005. "Materiality: An Introduction." In *Materiality,* edited by Daniel Miller, 1–50. Durham, NC: Duke University Press.

Moran, Anna, and Sorcha O'Brien. 2014. "Editors' Foreword." In *Love Objects: Emotion, Design and Material Culture,* edited by Anna Moran and Sorcha O'Brien, xiii–xv. London: Bloomsbury.

Muñoz, José Esteban. 2009. "Introduction: Feeling Utopia." In *Cruising Utopia: The Politics and Performance of Queer Futurity*, 1–32. New York: New York University Press.

Murray, Stephen O., and Will Roscoe. 1997. *Islamic Homosexualities: Culture, History, and Literature.* New York: New York University Press.

Nancy, Jean-Luc. 2007. *Listening.* Translated by Charlotte Mandell. New York: Fordham University Press.

Navaro-Yashin, Yael. 2009. "Affective Spaces, Melancholic Objects: Ruination and the Production of Anthropological Knowledge." *Journal of the Royal Anthropological Institute* 15 (1): 1–18.

Nietzsche, Friedrich. 1997. "Sanctus Januarius (Selections) from the Gay Science (1882/87)." In *Philosophical Writings*, edited by Reinhold Grimm and Caroline Molina y Vedia, 139–59. New York: Continuum.

Nordstrom, Carolyn. 1998. "Deadly Myths of Aggression." *Aggressive Behaviour* 24 (2): 147–59.

Novak, David, and Matt Sakakeeny. 2015. "Introduction." In *Keywords in Sound*, edited by David Novak and Matt Sakakeeny, 1–12. Durham, NC: Duke University Press.

Ochoa Gautier, Ana María. 2015. "Silence." In *Keywords in Sound*, edited by David Novak and Matt Sakakeeny, 183–92. Durham, NC: Duke University Press.

Ouzgane, Lahoucine. 2006. "Islamic Masculinities: An Introduction." In *Islamic Masculinities*, edited by L. Ouzgane, 1–8. London: Zed Books.

Özyürek, Esra. 2006. *Nostalgia for the Modern: State Secularism and Everyday Politics in Turkey.* Durham, NC: Duke University Press.

Parpart, Jane, and Marysia Zalewski. 2008. *Re-thinking the Man Question: Sex, Gender and Violence in International Relations.* London: Zed Press.

Peteet, Julie. M. 1994. "Male Gender and Rituals of Resistance in the Palestinian Intifada: A Cultural Politics of Violence." *American Ethnologist* 21 (1): 31–49.

———. 1997. "Icons and Militants: Mothering in the Danger Zone." *Signs* 23: 103–29.

————. 2007. "Problematizing a Palestinian Diaspora." *International Journal of Middle East Studies* 39 (4): 6274–76.

Pinney, Christopher. 2005. "Things Happen; or, From Which Moment Does That Object Come?" In *Materiality*, edited by Daniel Miller, 256–72. Durham, NC: Duke University Press.

Potter, Caroline. 2008. "Sense of Motion, Senses of Self: Becoming a Dancer." *Ethnos* 73 (4): 444–65.

Povrzanović Frykman, Maja. 2016. "Sensitive Objects of Humanitarian Aid: Corporeal Memories and Affective Continuities" In *Sensitive Objects: Affect and Material Culture*, edited by Jonas Frykman and Maja Povrzanović Frykman, 79–106. Lund: Nordic Academic Press.

Protevi, John. 2009. *Political Affect: Connecting the Social and the Somatic.* Minneapolis: University of Minnesota Press.

Purbrick, Louise. 2014. "'I Love Giving Presents': The Emotion of Material Culture." In *Love Objects: Emotion, Design and Material Culture*, edited by Anna Moran and Sorcha O'Brien, 9–20. London: Bloomsbury.

Rabo, Annika. 1996. "Gender, State, and Civil Society in Jordan and Syria." In *Civil Society: Challenging Western Models*, edited by Elizabeth Dunn and Chris Hann, 155–77. London: Routledge.

Renshaw, Layla. 2010. "Missing Bodies Near-at-Hand: The Dissonant Memory and Dormant Graves of the Spanish Civil War." In *An Anthropology of Absence: Materializations of Transcendence and Loss*, edited by Mikkel Bille, Frida Hastrup, and Tim Flohr, 45–61. London: Springer.

Rhani, Zakaria. 2013. In *Affective Politics in Transitional North Africa: Imagining the Future*, edited by Maria Frederika Malmström. Workshop and Roundtable Report, Conflict, Displacement and Transformation conference proceedings, May 27–28, 2013, Alexandria, Egypt. Uppsala: The Nordic Africa Institute. Accessed June 20, 2015. http://nai.diva-portal.org/smash/get/diva2:693357/FULLTEXT01.pdf.

Robins, Alexander. 2014. "Peirce and Photography: Art, Semiotics, and Science." *The Journal of Speculative Philosophy* 28 (1): 1–16.

Rommel, Carl. 2015. "Revolution, Play and Feeling, Assembling Emotionality, National Subjectivity and Football in Cairo, 1990–2013."

PhD diss., Department of Anthropology and Sociology, SOAS, University of London.

Saad, Mohammed. 2013. "Arts Academy Director Starts War against Morsi-Appointed Culture Minister." *Ahram Online*, May 14. Accessed May 14, 2013. http://english.ahram.org.eg/NewsContent/5/35/71401/Arts--Culture/Stage--Street/Arts-academy-director-starts-war-against-Morsiappo.aspx.

Schafer, R. Murray. 1977. *The Tuning of the World*. New York: Knopf.

Schielke, Samuli. 2015. *Egypt in the Future Tense: Hope, Frustration, and Ambivalence before and after 2011*. Bloomington: Indiana University Press.

Scott, David. 2014. *Omens of Adversity: Tragedy, Time, Memory, Justice*. Durham, NC: Duke University Press.

Sedgwick, Eve Kosofsky. 2003. *Touching Feeling: Affect, Pedagogy, Performativity*. Durham, NC: Duke University Press.

Sharabi, Hisham. 1992. *Neopatriarchy: A Theory of Distorted Change in Arab Society*. Oxford: Oxford University Press.

Shouse, Eric. 2005. "Feeling, Emotion, Affect." *M/C Journal* 8, no. 6. Accessed May 11, 2017. http://journal.media-culture.org.au/0512/03-shouse.php.

Singerman, Diane, and Homa Hoodfar. 1996. "Introduction: The Infitah, Development and Gendered Change." In *Development, Change, and Gender in Cairo: A View from Household*, edited by Diane Singerman and Homa Hoodfar, xi–xl. Bloomington: Indiana University Press.

Škrbić Alempijević, Nevena, and Sanja Potkonjak. 2016. "The Titoaffect. Tracing Objects and Memories of Socialism in Postsocialist Croatia." In *Sensitive Objects: Affect and Material Culture*, edited by Jonas Frykman and Maja Povrzanović Frykman, 107–25. Lund: Nordic Academic Press.

Smith, Mark, ed. 2001. *Listening to Nineteenth-Century America*. Chapel Hill: University of North Carolina Press.

Sontag, Susan. 1977. *On Photography*. New York: Farrar, Straus and Giroux.

Stern, Maria, and Nystrand, Malin. 2006. "Gender and Armed Conflict." Stockholm: Sida. Accessed April 17, 2015. http://www.sida.se

/English/publications/Publication_database/Publications-by
-year/2006/april/Gender-and-Armed-Conflict/.

Stern, Maria, and Zalewski, Marysia. 2009. "Feminist Fatigue(s): Reflections on Feminist Fables of Militarization." *Review of International Studies* 35: 611–30.

Sterne, Jonathan. 2003. *The Audible Past: Cultural Origins of Sound Reproduction*. Durham, NC: Duke University Press.

———. 2012. *The Sound Studies Reader*. London: Routledge.

Stewart, Kathleen. 2007. *Ordinary Affects*. Durham, NC: Duke University Press.

Stokes, Martin. 2010. "Abd al-Halim's Microphone." In *Music and the Play of Power: Music, Politics and Ideology in the Middle East, North Africa and Central Asia,* edited by Laudan Nooshin, 55–75. London: Ashgate Press.

Stoler, Ann Laura. 2008. "Imperial Debris: Reflections on Ruins and Ruination." *Cultural Anthropology* 23 (2): 191–219.

Thompson, Emily. 2002. *The Soundscape of Modernity: Architectural Acoustics and the Culture of Listening in America, 1900–1933*. Cambridge, MA: MIT Press.

Trovalla, Eric, and Ulrika Trovalla. 2015. "Infrastructure Turned Suprastructure: Unpredictable Materialities and Visions of a Nigerian Nation." *Journal of Material Culture* 20 (1): 43–57.

Walsh, Declan. 2017 "Despite Public Outcry, Egypt to Transfer Islands to Saudi Arabia," Accessed April 3, 2018. *New York Times.* https://www.nytimes.com/2017/06/14/world/middleeast/egypt-saudi-arabia-islands-sisi.html.

Wiemann, Dirk, and Lars Eckstein. 2013. "Introduction: Towards a Cultural Politics of Passion." In *The Politics of Passion: Reframing Affect and Emotion in Global Modernity,* edited by Dirk Wiemann and Lars Eckstein, 7–34. Frankfurt am Maine: Peter Lang Academic Research.

Wilcox, Lauren B. 2015a. *Bodies of Violence: Theorizing Embodied Subjects in International Relations*. Oxford: Oxford University Press.

———. 2015b. Presentation at the Global IR and Regional Worlds, International Studies Association, 56th Annual Convention. New Orleans, February 18–21, 2015.

Winegar, Jessica. 2012. "The Privilege of Revolution: Gender, Class, Space, and Affect in Egypt." *American Ethnologist* 39 (1): 67–70.

———. 2014. "Ambiguous Symbols in the Egyptian Uprising." *Stanford University Press Blog.* January 21. Accessed June 22, 2015. http://stanfordpress.typepad.com/blog/2014/01/the-ambiguous-power-of-symbols-in-the-egyptian-uprising.html.

Wool, Zoë H., and Julie Livingston. 2017. Introduction. In "Collateral Afterworlds: Sociality Besides Redemption," ed. Zoë H. Wool and Julie Livingston, special issue, *Social Text* 35 (1): 1–15.

Index

Abdullah of Saudi Arabia,
  mourning of, 100, 117
Abell, Sam, 76
absences, 75–78; absent bodies,
  88–90; presence of, 75, 90
Aclimandos, Tewfik, 112
acoustic space, 57, 131. *See also* sound
actants, 8–9
aesthetic politics, 100, 101
affect: defined, 6–7; love and, 37–39,
  46, 49–50; materialities of, 9–10,
  93, 103–5; nondiscursive
  experience of, 117–19; photography and, 74–77; politics of, 1–6,
  9–12, 57–59, 65–66, 103–7, 118–19,
  123–24; silence as a new force of,
  117; theory of, 4–7, 58, 97;
  transmission of, xxii, 10–11, 15, 19,
  33–34, 38, 46, 78–79, 81, 117, 126
affective matter: agential force
  and, 74; gaze and, 73–75, 78;
  sit-ins and, 72–74; 83–86.
  See also thing-materialities;
  thinking-matter

affective responses: aesthetic
  politics and, 100; masculinities
  and, 101; place and, 19–20, 39–41,
  45–46, 53; rifts in, 9; things and,
  45–46, 78–79
affect theory, 4–7, 58, 97
agency, 32, 79, 118; of the body, 15,
  39, 52; bio-aspect of, 89;
  masculinities and, 118, 132–35n2;
  material, 8–9, 74
agential capacity, 8–9, 90
agential force, 16, 74, 90
Ahmed, 21–26, 121–22
Al-Fath Mosque, 63–64
Al Jazeera, 59
al-Nahda Square, Cairo, 3, 16, 71,
  74–75, 85, 93–94, 98, 112–13
Amar, Paul, 106, 119
amor fati, 92–93
analysis, mode of, 7–11
Appadurai, Arjun, 119, 130n2
Arab Spring, 14, 113
Arab Winter, 15
artifact-oriented anthropology, 8

violence, 86, 93, 112–13, 120, 134;
abstract, 91; acoustic, 68;
certainty and, 119; infliction of
by the state (state-sponsored
violence) 54, 97; political, 69, 75,
91, 115; military, 133; social, 121;
sound of, 65

voyeurism, 75, 92

war: sounds of, 57–58, 62, 64, 66; on
terrorism, 4, 88, 98
weapons, 42
Wiemann, Dirk, 60, 103, 117
World Bank, 108

Founded in 1893,
UNIVERSITY OF CALIFORNIA PRESS
publishes bold, progressive books and journals
on topics in the arts, humanities, social sciences,
and natural sciences—with a focus on social
justice issues—that inspire thought and action
among readers worldwide.

The UC PRESS FOUNDATION
raises funds to uphold the press's vital role
as an independent, nonprofit publisher, and
receives philanthropic support from a wide
range of individuals and institutions—and from
committed readers like you. To learn more, visit
ucpress.edu/supportus.